DIVERSIFYING
DIPLOMACY

ADST-DACOR Diplomats and Diplomacy Series

SERIES EDITOR

Margery Boichel Thompson

Since 1776, extraordinary men and women have
represented the United States abroad under widely
varying circumstances. What they did and how
and why they did it remain little known to their
compatriots. In 1995, the Association for Diplomatic
Studies and Training (ADST) and DACOR, an
organization of foreign affairs professionals, created
the Diplomats and Diplomacy book series to
increase public knowledge and appreciation of the
professionalism of American diplomats and their
involvement in world history. The story of Harriet
Elam-Thomas's trajectory from growing up in the
Roxbury section of Boston to heading the U.S.
embassy in Dakar, Senegal, is the sixty-second
volume in the series.

DIVERSIFYING DIPLOMACY

My Journey from Roxbury to Dakar

Harriet Lee Elam-Thomas *with* Jim Robison

Foreword by Allan E. Goodman | Preface by John C. Bersia

Potomac Books | *An imprint of the University of Nebraska Press*

An ADST-DACOR Diplomats and Diplomacy Book

Publication of this volume was made possible in part by
the generous support of the H. Lee and Carol Gendler
Charitable Fund.

Library of Congress Cataloging-in-Publication Data
Names: Elam-Thomas, Harriet Lee, 1941– author. Robison,
Jim, 1952– author.
Title: Diversifying diplomacy: my journey from Roxbury to
Dakar / Harriet Lee Elam-Thomas with Jim Robison;
foreword by Allan Goodman; preface by John Bersia.
Description: Lincoln, Nebraska: Potomac Books, 2017.
Series: ADST-DACOR diplomats and diplomacy series
Includes index.
Identifiers: LCCN 2017026737 (print)
LCCN 2017044326 (ebook)
ISBN 9781612349800 (epub)
ISBN 9781612349817 (mobi)
ISBN 9781612349824 (pdf)
ISBN 9781612349503 (hardback: alk. paper)
Subjects: LCSH: Elam-Thomas, Harriet Lee, 1941– |
Diplomats—United States—Biography. | Women
diplomats—United States—Biography. | African Amer-
ican diplomats—Biography. | United States—Foreign
relations—Senegal. | Senegal—Foreign relations—United
States. | United States—Foreign relations—1989– | BISAC:
BIOGRAPHY & AUTOBIOGRAPHY / Women. | BIOGRAPHY &
AUTOBIOGRAPHY / Political. | POLITICAL SCIENCE / Inter-
national Relations / Diplomacy.
Classification: LCC E840.8.E43 (ebook) | LCC E840.8.E43 A3
2017 (print) | DDC 327.2092 [B]—dc23
LC record available at https://lccn.loc.gov/2017026737

Set in Adobe Caslon.

Contents

Illustrations

Foreword

ALLAN E. GOODMAN

"You really need to interview her." This advice from the head of the U.S. Information Agency's (USIA) Equal Employment Opportunity Office made it clear that Harriet Elam had succeeded. She was in line to become the senior-most Foreign Service officer at the agency. She would soon be its counselor. And, many said, an ambassadorship would be next.

I was struck initially by the character of her office. It was grand as government offices go and clearly thought out. A visitor would see the traces of service abroad, commendations, and above all, that it was just neat and proper. What Harriet did not know is that the head of personnel had just given me a tour of the old USIA/Voice of America headquarters. The Wilbur J. Cohen Building had been constructed in 1940 and contained some famous Ben Shahn murals, depicting the era of the New Deal.

But my attention was directed to two water fountains. A few feet separated them. "Remember," I was told, "the U.S. government used to be segregated. It started with Woodrow Wilson. We had separate bathrooms and still have these separate fountains." I found their continued existence, this particular lesson in history, strange.

Harriet would give me another, more pleasant lesson that day when I made a casual remark about how elegant her office appeared. I expected she would give me the tour of where she had been for each of the pictures and artifacts displayed. Instead, she said what made the office nice for her and others on the executive floor was how hard the cleaning staff worked to keep things clean. "We all work pretty late into the evening. And only when we go home do the cleaners get to start their work. It isn't easy, and I am grateful to them every morning I come back in."

Over the next twenty-five years, I would learn a lot from Harriet.

The date of our first encounter was 1995. I had been asked by the director of the USIA, Joe Duffey, to conduct an independent study of the diversity of the USIA Foreign Service personnel and to determine if the agency offered equality of opportunity in promotions, salary, and awards. The Foreign Service Act of 1980 had mandated that equality and required that "the members of America's Foreign Service should be representative of the American people."

The report I submitted later was entitled "Separate and Unequal." I had found that at virtually every level in the service and at every opportunity to be recognized for an award, I would not want to change the color of my white skin. Sadly, I found that some on duty also regarded it as important that the two water fountains be kept as they were, saying so openly. I found much worse. These same officers advanced much faster in their careers, despite behavior and attitudes that should have no place in our public service today, no matter what President Wilson did or thought in his time.

Harriet's book is about what people can achieve and do when they do not look like me. And what we all can learn by their stories and their leadership.

Our Declaration of Independence, citing "a decent respect to the opinions of mankind," recognizes an American trait, a need to explain things. We believe telling our story is important. We need able diplomats who can do this to the many audiences at places where most of the people do not look like me. Although I do not know the exact level of diversity in the Foreign Service today, I am fairly sure we are still far from the goal Congress intended. We need more people like Harriet, people willing to devote their lives to a difficult task. This book ought to inspire as well as inform. It does for me.

As Harriet notes, diplomats need "a mixture of empathy, persuasion, bluster, and courage." Amen. They also need to be able to light up a room when they speak and to remember to thank those who came to hear them—and those who will clean up and turn out the lights after everyone else has gone home.

Over the course of my travels, I have actually met many of the local staff who served with Harriet in her various posts. They speak of her with appreciation and a certain reverence, not because she achieved so much or rose so high but because she never forgot her roots or the role Foreign Service nationals played in contributing to her success.

One lesson from this book is that it is sometimes the little things that contribute importantly to the decent regard people have for us and that this aspect of diplomacy pays dividends over many years. As this book so eloquently reports, the girl from Roxbury did exceptionally well at representing us all.

Preface

Although a book's preface is typically written by its author, I welcome the opportunity to describe how this particular work came into being, having attentively observed its development. For more than a decade, I listened to comments made by those in Harriet Elam-Thomas's circle—from her husband, Wilfred J. Thomas, and longtime friends in the Washington DC, Maryland, and Virginia area to newer friends, colleagues, and students in Central Florida—as to why she should write a book. For much of that time, she reacted with disbelief, followed by a question: What might she have to say that would differ from the many memoirs written by diplomatic colleagues with similar or even greater accomplishments? The answer, as readers will shortly realize, plays out beautifully in the following pages.

One of the first to encourage Ambassador Elam-Thomas was Olive Kelsey, a colleague and friend she met in Paris a half century ago. Another was Milton Coleman, who took the time to send her a lengthy email message a decade back outlining the impact such a book could have on young people of any hue contemplating a career in international affairs. Closer to home, her husband regularly urged her to share the challenges and successes in her career to demonstrate to young men and women that they, too, could reach the highest ranks of the diplomatic service. Orlando-based friends such as Beverly Marshall-Luney and Dan Haggerty later joined the chorus. I quietly applauded their enthusiasm, for I knew they were right.

Then students in Ambassador Elam-Thomas's honors diplomacy course at the University of Central Florida (UCF) added their voices, encouraging her to preserve some of the many stories she related in class to illustrate effective ways of building lasting relationships across cultures. Why not chronicle her journey from Simmons College, with a degree in international business, to work as a secretary in the U.S. embassy in Paris, her time in President Richard Nixon's White House, her first State Department posting in Dakar as an assistant cultural affairs officer, and eventually her return to Dakar twenty-eight years later as the U.S. ambassador to the Republic of Senegal?

She learned French as a teenager, Greek at the age of forty-two, and—inspired by witnessing a speech by South Africa's former president, Nelson Mandela—Turkish at forty-seven. Those linguistic talents served her well, for she spent seventeen years of her career dealing with Greece, Turkey, and Cyprus. There was much more to come. Never in her wildest dreams did she think she would later serve as counselor of the U.S. Information Agency, the organization's senior-most career officer, for the two years prior to its integration into the Department of State. Nor did she imagine she would find herself on a stage with Secretary of State Madeleine Albright and Assistant Secretary Evelyn Lieberman on October 1, 1999, as they presided over the ceremony during which she handed the "keys of USIA" to Secretary Albright. That event took place two days before she married Wilfred. The *Washington Post* reported, "Harriet Elam will have a busy weekend." Busy it was and truly life changing, as well.

This book is designed primarily to inform readers about Ambassador Elam-Thomas's forty-two-year career in the Foreign Service as an honest and authentic representative of the United States. The memoir also covers the dozen years that followed, first as a diplomat in residence (an opportunity I was proud to initiate through UCF's partnership with the Department of State), then as a professor-advisor and director of the Diplomacy Program at UCF. There she navigated the delicate balance of teaching the practical aspects of diplomacy while respecting the importance of history and theory.

In addition, this book serves to remind those who have only documentaries and Hollywood versions of diplomatic life that it is not all cocktail parties and receptions. Diplomacy is a profession filled with trials as well as triumphs. Those trials have increased exponentially with accelerated globalization and all it entails.

In closing, I invite readers to follow the journey of Harriet Elam-Thomas, "the little Elam girl from Roxbury," who went on not only to shoulder some of the world's heftier problems but also to ensure—through her students and others who draw inspiration from her memoir—that new shepherds of honesty and authenticity will trace her international footsteps for generations to come.

Acknowledgments

Without the unceasing commitment of my coauthor Jim Robison, a respected Florida historian, author, and journalist, we would not have the detailed chronology of my ancestry. We would not have the accurate references to the diplomatic history noted herein. My big brother Judge Harry's memoir provided the core traditions of the Elam family, which shaped my life and ethics. Without Jim Dandridge's patience as I responded to questioning during his more than eleven hours of my oral history interview, we would not have the essential details of my foreign and domestic assignments. Without the first readers, Wilfred Thomas, Olive Kelsey, and Patricia Ambinder, I could not pass the work on for others to edit. Christopher Datta tops that list, for he did yeoman work on the umpteenth draft. A consummate diplomat and published writer, Chris reminded me of important grammar lessons I had forgotten. He also provided the missing critical eye with respect to the challenges during the integration of USIA to State.

Because he recognized the impact of facts and accurate figures, my husband, Wilfred, researched the number and then calculated the percentage of African American women who served as chief of mission. Wilfred, who still calculates complex figures in his head, wanted to show me why it was important for me to write this book. He was right. The percentage was so low that it proved the point that his spouse was part of a distinctive circle of African American women who served as career ambassadors.

My very special thanks go to my Global Perspective colleagues, beginning with John Bersia and Jessica Squires, who gave me continuous support throughout this process. A special shout out to Rick Bronson, associate instructor at UCF's Nicholson School of Communications, for his guidance early on. I am grateful that UCF gave me the flexibility needed to devote significant time to this effort. My heartfelt gratitude to Abeer Abdalla, one of the first UCF students who constantly reminded me of the need to write this book and read early portions. A very special *merci beaucoup* to Richard Haddock, one of our interns, who reviewed forty-two years of my personal files and placed them in chronological order. Nataya Pihtayanukul earns my thanks as well for her initial editing of my oral history, which served as the basis for this work.

It has been my goal throughout the writing of this book to entice readers to enjoy the journey of "the Little Elam girl from Roxbury" that I have had the joy to live and now to share.

DIVERSIFYING
DIPLOMACY

Introduction

America's Approach Is Not the Planet's Only Game

The United States must produce enough citizens with critical skills to fill the ranks of the Foreign Service, the intelligence community, and the armed forces. For the United States to maintain its military and diplomatic leadership role, it needs highly qualified and capable men and women to conduct its foreign affairs.
—ALLAN E. GOODMAN, Institute of International Education, May 21, 2012

Growing up in Boston, in my downsized version of the world, I used to wrinkle my face when neighbors referred to me as the "little Elam girl," because my siblings were seventeen to twenty years my senior. Later, when my career decisions thrust me into an outsized version of the world as a globe-trotting diplomat, I no longer harbored such worries. Indeed, a smile usually accompanied my reflections on my early, simpler life.

Thus I begin a story that traces the modern diplomatic history of the United States through my own experience. It is a story of careful listening, artful speaking, attentive observing, respectful gesturing, and creative striving to shape lasting connections across cultures and customs. And it is a story in which I have been studiously engaged.

Bear in mind that I did not come from a family of privilege. My parents left their home states in the segregated Old South to raise a family in Massachusetts. What they lacked in education, they made up for in wisdom and determination—traits that they instilled in their children. My early experiences as a foreign exchange student living in the home of a music teacher in France during the U.S. civil rights movement ignited my desire to undertake the challenges of helping to improve America's image abroad.

Today, I am more aware than ever that nothing of life in America escapes notice in other nations. Decisions made in the White House, the halls of Congress, and the Pentagon, as well as at what one colleague calls the "comfy digs in Arlington" of the Department of State's Foreign Service Institute affect lives across the planet. U.S. global reach stretches into countries most Americans would not even know existed.

My own part in this international adventure was highlighted by a president's nomination—with the advice and consent of the Senate—for me to serve as an ambassador. When I served as the U.S. ambassador to Senegal, my duties also included responsibility for its southern neighbor, the Republic of Guinea-Bissau, a small coastal nation whose people rank among the poorest in the world. During my tenure in Dakar, the foreign national staff was predominantly Senegalese, but there were others from Guinea-Bissau, Togo, and Lebanon. All worked very well together. Senegal is a predominantly Muslim nation. However, Léopold Sédar Senghor—the country's first president after independence—was Catholic. Embassy staff celebrated, and continue to celebrate, Christian and Muslim holidays. Interfaith and interracial marriages are not unusual.

Senegal may not be as well known as Rwanda, Liberia, Sierra Leone, Guinea, and some other African nations, perhaps because it has not experienced a coup, devastating health crises, or targeting by terrorists. Yet Senegal and Guinea-Bissau are among the nearly two hundred countries maintaining political, economic, and cultural relations with the United States.

I decided to write this book after my forty-two-year career in the U.S. Foreign Service. Following the completion of my three-year tour in Senegal, my husband and I settled in Leesburg, Florida, thanks to his preference for warmer climates. The other incentive was my new assignment as the State Department's first diplomat in residence (DIR) at the University of Central Florida (UCF), a state institution located in Orlando. I arrived at my quarters in the university's Global

Perspectives Office in March 2003. This environment allowed me to continue my global engagement and share my Foreign Service expertise with a curious and excited new student audience. It was the ideal transition to follow my time in Dakar, Senegal.

My host, John C. Bersia, a Pulitzer Prize–winning journalist and educator, is UCF president John C. Hitt's special assistant for global perspectives. Since 2001, Bersia has endeavored to fulfill Hitt's vision to develop UCF's global resources, capabilities, and connections, thereby sharpening the international focus of what is now the second largest university in the United States. Though my initial assignment as DIR was for a year, at Hitt's request, I remained for a second year. The DIR assignment led to my accepting an appointment as director to establish a diplomacy program at the university. By the time this memoir is published, my UCF connection will have spanned fourteen years.

The DIR Program is designed to reach out to students who might not be aware of the existence of foreign affairs careers in the U.S. government. In general, students attending Ivy League, globally focused universities have been well represented in the U.S. diplomatic service. Reaching beyond those institutions is essential, though, for the Department of State to realize its goal of a truly diverse Foreign Service that looks like all of America. Cultural competence and diversity bring a much broader perspective of the United States, which is critical to enhancing mutual understanding in today's world.

In the classroom, at speaking opportunities, and in the pages of this book, I draw on life experiences that have shaped my worldview. As I tell my students, the most effective Foreign Service officers come with a view of the world and its diverse cultures that is wide open and accepting. Travel abroad certainly counts, but the exchange experience of living with a family in my junior year of college was invaluable. It was a life-enhancing experience that a touristic visit could never have matched. Through this in-depth exchange experience, I became more sensitive to and tolerant of differences, and also less judgmental. Priorities changed.

Regarding my private life as a diplomat, for all except the final few years of my Foreign Service career, I remained single. This was a personal choice, no doubt influenced by the fact that—until the 1970s—women who married were expected to leave the Foreign Service. As I told the editors of *Onyx* magazine in 2013, the State Department, as an institution, did not embrace women until a class action suit was filed. Before 1971, not only were women in the Foreign Service unable to marry, they were not given the opportunity to serve as political counselors or economic counselors in embassies abroad. Changing this mind-set has been a process. I am thankful to former secretary of state Madeleine Albright for sending back a list for ambassadorial assignments because it did not include enough women.

Whenever I encountered colleagues in diplomatic settings, they were usually men. I saw very few women—and even fewer women of color. Wearing a skirt in the Foreign Service was ten times more difficult than having brown skin. Few of my colleagues looked like me. Although I do not profess to have been an effective diplomat because of my race, ethnicity, or gender, I believe these elements of my persona paid dividends. Though I thoroughly prepared for each new assignment, I am certain the key to making a contribution toward a credible articulation of U.S. foreign policy was the fact that I had the opportunity to serve and felt included. Without inclusion, all of the lip service to diversity would have been suspect.

By the time I left the State Department, I had acquired three foreign languages, developed detailed knowledge of a host of different cultures, learned to listen and hear others, and gained the ability to speak with far more sensitivity. I had also learned to include significant aspects of each of the cultures I encountered in my decision making during my assignments.

Writer Peggy Tabor Millin, a close observer of the human condition, once watched wind push raindrops across a window. Separate drops merged and then split apart, each carrying with it a part of the other. People and cultures are like that, too. They touch one another and are forever changed by the experience. No matter where we are, no matter what we are doing in the United States or abroad, "we never touch people so lightly that we do not leave a trace," Millin tells us.

To listen, use words with care, observe attentively before speaking, show respect for other people, and remain sensitive to our tone of voice or body language will result in a positive image that allows for the creation of lasting connections across cultures and customs.

Nancy Hoepli-Phalon, a former Foreign Policy Association editor, describes America's foreign policy as "the expression of its goals in the world and of how it proposes to achieve them. It is a reflection of the nation's interests, the most basic of which are sovereignty and independence." To those, she adds democracy, economic security, protection of human rights, and environmental security.

Many of my colleagues have said that a diplomat needs a mixture of empathy, persuasion, bluster, and courage, with the goal of keeping channels of communication open, defusing tension, and averting violence. Since the end of World War II, more ambassadors than generals have died serving their country in foreign lands. American diplomats make that choice, sometimes finding themselves in harm's way, but knowing that they cannot work solely behind the walls of secure embassies. Instead, they must promote American policies by engaging with the people and the cultures of their assigned countries. All of those entering the Foreign Service make the same choice, accepting that every few years they will be uprooted and reassigned to an entirely new land away from home. And, as the headlines reveal, serving your country overseas is sometimes a dangerous choice.

Three of my U.S. Information Agency (USIA) colleagues were among the embassy hostages held in Iran for more than 444 days. My driver in Turkey found a bomb under the car next to mine as I was leaving a performance of Mozart's *The Abduction from the Seraglio* at Topkapi Palace in Istanbul. Projectiles were tossed at my office window at the consulate annex, which was right next to the famous Pera Palace Hotel, where Agatha Christie wrote *Murder on the Orient Express*.

Accepting that most of his or her career will be spent away from home, a diplomat must have an insatiable curiosity and expanding knowledge of not just his or her own county and its foreign policies but the history, cultures, and needs of many other countries. Jack Zetkulic, a seasoned diplomat, counsels young Foreign Service officers on this point, calling preparations for assignments "fireproofing." He cautions, "You do not want to get hosed" by your host-country counterparts, "most of whom will have a solid knowledge of American history and international relations."

Perhaps a successful diplomat's most useful talent is an enthusiasm to engage others, often in a language and setting foreign to one's comforts. The best leaders are sincere and humble. Real leadership has to do with integrity and performance; neither one can take a holiday. They reflect on your character and soul. On June 26, 1990, I sat with rapt attention in the Senate gallery when former South African president Nelson Mandela, the quintessential leader, addressed a joint session of Congress after his release from prison. I was inspired. He was a master at seeking consensus, and he believed in the human heart. We can all learn from his example. I credit Mandela's stirring presentation for motivating me to pass a Turkish-language exam, which I took two weeks later.

Our culture is one that often speaks rather than listens. I might not always practice what I preach, but I know that listening is the most effective approach to meaningful dialogue in any setting. Listening is an art. When someone speaks, it is important to give him or her your undivided attention. We need to listen not only to the spoken words but to the unspoken messages. This means looking directly at a person and making eye contact. We need to forget we are wearing a watch and just focus on that person for a moment. It is called respect. It is called appreciation. It is called anticipation. And it is called leadership.

By listening, one can learn another's values. And here is where learning other languages becomes critical, as it leads to a deeper, mutual understanding and appreciation. This has been true for me, my colleagues, and those with whom I have engaged in other nations. Listening attentively and speaking in another's language enhances communication.

Tone of voice, body language, and word choice expose attitudes. I like to remind my students that the British do not drive on the wrong side of the road. A less judgmental statement would be that the British drive on the other side of the road. Similarly, we should not say Arabic is written backward but rather that Arabic is written from right to left. Further, we should not make disparaging remarks about the languages and foods of another country or culture. I also remind my students that maps in other parts of the world do not necessarily show the continent of North America in the middle. We might be accustomed to seeing such a depiction on many U.S. classroom maps, which may account for why we incorrectly assume we are at the center of the universe.

In our diplomatic work abroad, we are not selling a product. In public diplomacy, we are dealing with human relations and social patterns, and that requires a very different approach, along with a sense of sincerity in our interaction and dialogue with those who relay our views to a foreign government.

Americans often think they can quickly win friends and influence people just because they are American. But people of other cultures are routinely steeped in history, and they respect the value of what transpired in their past. They build upon that history to make decisions. First of all, we do not have the same kind of history. Our country is not that old. It can be difficult for Americans to grasp that we are still relative youngsters in a world of countries with cultural histories that stretch back centuries before the founding of colonial America. At the same time, an American diplomat must present an accurate view of the United States and the multicultural, adaptive, and acculturated life of Americans.

It is also worth emphasizing that America is not the only hub of diplomacy in the world. There are talented, incredibly well-versed communicators from every part of the globe. In 1971, at the very beginning of my career, I was a member of the U.S. delegation to the twenty-fifth United Nations General Assembly. As the program officer for youth, students, and special programs at the State Department in the Bureau of Educational and Cultural Affairs, I sat in awe listening to delegates from the Caribbean, Asia, and Latin America. They were able to expound upon their countries' positions in a language that often was not their mother tongue, and to do so as well as, if not more convincingly than, some of our own representatives. One of the most impressive figures from that time was Keith Johnson, Jamaica's ambassador to the United Nations, who served his country for more than fifty years in the diplomatic service.

Years later, when I was posted in Greece, I prepared a two-year study of that country's educational system. I encountered certain Greek students who were as well educated as their American counterparts and in some cases even more advanced. Neither the American education system nor the Greek one is perfect. Far from it. Yet I learned that through objectivity, perspective, openness, and listening—especially listening—I was able to gain additional knowledge and perspective.

I have also learned from other humbling experiences as an American delegate to international organizations. As a counselor of USIA from 1997 to 1999, I joined our U.S. delegation to a United Nations Educational, Scientific and Cultural Organization (UNESCO) meeting in Stockholm. At that time, the United States had pulled out of UNESCO because we had become dissatisfied with the secretary general's management of the organization. We attended the meeting with "observer status," which meant, though nonmembers, we were able to state our positions from the back of the room. The Vatican was also an observer, but its delegates were accustomed to this seating arrangement. I remember thinking it was a very good experience for my State Department colleagues, for now they finally understood the feeling of not always being seated at the head of the table.

In Stockholm, the audience was attentive to our statements because, after all, we still represented the United States. I counseled our delegation members to comport themselves carefully—and avoid a heavy-handed approach and forceful language—if we wanted to insert our wording or have our views reflected in the final communiqué. Our State Department colleague, E. Michael Southwick, made the presentation. A career diplomat and later ambassador to Uganda, he devoted his thirty-six-year career to working with African nations on conflict resolution and development issues. The Stockholm UNESCO conference provided me with close access to world leaders, including lengthy sidebar discussions with a respected colleague from my time in Istanbul, Dr. Ekmeleddin İhsanoğlu, who headed the Organization of Islamic Conference. He subsequently became a 2014 candidate for prime minister in Turkey.

If we are to foster a sincere diplomatic connection with someone from Iran, Iraq, France, or another country, we must first establish credible personal relationships that take time and require patience to nurture. Such meetings offer that unique opportunity.

Many one-of-a-kind encounters have taught me that meaningful domestic and international communication comes about only when we truly listen to others with whom we sometimes have serious disagreements. All of us want to be understood and not misinterpreted based on what the news media have promoted about our culture. We Americans are not reflections of internationally popular television series such as *Dynasty* in the 1980s or the latest "reality" TV shows. Despite the abundance of entertainment produced by Hollywood suggesting the contrary, Americans have moral values. Education plays an important role. The formal arts and plastic/creative arts build character. Our recent involvement in many conflict zones around the world has shown us that most societies seek basic human rights, and they recognize the value of culture in developing the mind and spirit.

I wish to emphasize how much I have benefited from the strong influence of my mentors, both family and professional. My hope is that, through my conduct, I can pass along the importance of discipline, hard work, integrity, and authenticity. I have been pleasantly surprised by the impact I have had on others. In the last few years, former students and Foreign Service colleagues have been in touch to bring me up to date on their lives. These are individuals who, for one reason or another, I imagined would not remember me.

Many individuals who might or might not be cited in this work have had singular impacts on my life. Without their patience, tolerance, candor, and sincere kindness, I might not have survived the many challenges of a Foreign Service career, navigated the landscape of academia as a professor and program director, or remained a sensitive human being. They are ever present today in my heart, and they nourish my soul. Despite this world of enormous heartbreak and challenges—and I am routinely reminded of them via twenty-four-hour, sobering newscasts—I am elated to have had opportunities to enrich people in foreign lands and at home with a distinctive view of the world and its peoples that I have come to know.

Today, unlike the early days of my career, diverse women of all hues represent this country overseas and elsewhere. Some have called this development the "Hillary Effect." But well before Hillary Clinton, our most recent female secretary of state, there was Madeleine Albright, the first woman to serve in that capacity, in 1997, and Condoleezza Rice, who served in that post from 2005 until 2009. And, beginning at a more junior posting in the Department of State in 1971, there was "the little Elam girl" from Boston.

I

What a Family!

I was born under the sign of the phoenix [the symbol of Atlanta]. I grew up under the sign of the phoenix. I always believed that from ashes you could make beautiful things, from chaos you could make peace, and from despair you could bring happiness. —RUTH A. DAVIS, in 2003 the highest-ranking African American woman in the State Department

Some African societies separate family into two groups, the *sasha*, for the living and recently deceased, and the *zamani*, those revered people from past generations who lived during a time before anyone alive today. My life's story cannot be told without honoring the memories of my *sasha* family and the legacies of my family's venerated *zamani*.

And what a family!

In January 2000, Wilfred, my husband of three months, and I arrived in Senegal's capital city of Dakar at the southern point of the rocky, triangle-shaped Cap Vert Peninsula, the westernmost tip of Africa. Within a few days, Wilfred and I walked out of the ambassador's residence in Fann, the suburban area of Dakar where most of the ministers and diplomats lived. A chauffeur-driven, four-door black limousine awaited to whisk us to Senegal's palace, where I would present my credentials to President Abdou Diouf. Our driver took us along the palm-lined boulevard that fronts the white sandy beaches of the Atlantic coast, past stunning ocean-front residences of nationals, American expatriates, and other international families, and then along the Corniche, where Senegalese carpenters, furniture makers, and artists displayed their wares. The car drove by the multistoried ministry buildings to the Palais de la République in the Plateau district at the peninsula's eastern coastline.

Due east of the palace is Senegal's reminder of the West African role in the Atlantic slave trade, the island of Gorée, with its Door of No Return, where in June 2013 President Barack Obama stood in wordless contemplation. Presidents Bill Clinton and George W. Bush, too, had visited Gorée during their terms in office.

Security cleared traffic as we traveled along the Route de la Corniche Ouest, normally a heavily traveled thoroughfare of this busy metropolitan city, with 2.5 million diverse residents and one of the largest seaports and industrial centers of West Africa. Dakar is the cultured French-speaking capital of West Africa, with an international feel, highlighted by its Avenue des Ambassadeurs for its many diplomatic missions.

On this day, I was holding up traffic. I thought to myself that the other drivers caught in gridlock must "love" waiting for my entourage to pass. I had been briefed that cross-city driving, even on good days, was one of the most frustrating facts of life in this city that shares more than its language with the chaotic drivers of Paris. Adding to the clogged roads was the intense heat just prior to the beginning of the mid-January rainy season in Dakar. After what seemed like an eternity, the driver turned onto Boulevard de la République and the final few blocks of the modern, high-rise city, to Avenue du Pr. L. Sédar Senghor and the Palais Présidentiel. I had been silent for the twenty-minute drive. My husband turned and faced me, commenting that he had never seen me so quiet. I pointed out the window to the outriders, in their red and black uniforms, on their motorcycles on each side of us. And on each side of the hood, flags waved, the Stars and Stripes on the right fender and, on the left fender, the dark blue flag with thirteen white stars circling the eagle coat of arms of the ambassadorial standard.

Somewhere along that drive it hit me: in just a few moments I would enter the Palais Présidentiel to present my letter of credence, signed by President Bill Clinton. How incredible. Oh my heavens, I really had left that little Boston girl behind! I never imaged this would happen. Sure, I had given an alumni speech at Simmons College a long time ago, in 1977, when I said someday I would like to be an ambassador, never, ever thinking I might achieve it.

What would Blanche and Robert Elam think if they were alive on this day? Their youngest child is going to see the head of a West African nation to represent the president of the United States of America. Just the realization of that moment overwhelmed me with a sense of history and the reassuring warmth of my place in my family's legacy.

Back in Boston, some seven decades before, Mrs. Theresa Dempsey, one of my parents' close friends, had called me "the flower of the flock." Of course, this did not please my sister (almost seventeen when I was born), for, until my late arrival, she was the "apple of my father's eye."

My brothers and sister used to put a sign on the carriage whenever one of them had to take me out for a stroll. It read, "This is my baby sister!" Back in those days, teenagers, male or female, seen pushing a stroller with a baby who might have been theirs might as well have been wearing a scarlet letter. My siblings said they did this to prevent the inevitable community gossip concerning the origin of this new addition to the Elam family.

Born September 15, 1941, I was the youngest of five children, all born in or near Boston, Massachusetts. My three brothers were born between 1920 and 1923. My sister came along in 1925. My parents were from the South. My great-grandparents on both sides of the family, and perhaps my grandparents, were slaves or first-generation freedmen and freedwomen in Virginia and South Carolina. My father, Robert Harry Elam, was born in Chase City, Virginia; my mother, Blanche Delnora Lee, was from Aiken, South Carolina.

Even now, more than sixty years since the Supreme Court's ruling in *Brown v. Board of Education* and the civil rights movement of the 1960s, which ended legal segregation, it is easy to see why the legacy of Jim Crow persuaded my family and others to move to the North to raise their children.

My grandfather on my father's side was named Greeg Elam, born in the 1860s. He followed the tradition of the times to use the family name of the white plantation owner. Virginia and other southern states had long treated blacks as property. Births were part of a plantation's business records, which were often incomplete and vague and many of which have been lost to history. No family Bible that might have listed his birth has survived. He lived and worked in the tobacco-farming area of south central Virginia near the spot where Mecklenburg, Lunenburg, and Charlotte Counties come together. The farmland where he lived was in Mecklenburg County on Virginia's southern border with North Carolina. The nearest town would become Chase City, some eighty miles southwest of Richmond. Chase City, incorporated by northerners in 1873, was named for the politically ambitious abolitionist Salmon P. Chase of Ohio, secretary of the treasury in Abraham Lincoln's cabinet and later chief justice of the Supreme Court. Beginning as a colony for United Presbyterians following the Civil War, Chase City's origins are firmly planted in the Reconstruction Era.

My grandfather married a woman known to us only as Lucy. They had five children, including my father, Robert Harry Elam, born on August 6, 1891. (For most of my dad's life, he thought his birthday was August 4. When my parents applied for their passports to visit me in Paris, we learned that the birth date recorded was two days later. We continued to celebrate his birthday on the fourth, for at that stage in his life it did not make sense to change.) My grandparents lived their entire lives in Chase City, near the south fork of the Meherrin River, which today divides Mecklenburg County from Lunenburg County.

Founded on February 26, 1763, Mecklenburg County was named for the German principality of Mecklenburg-Strelitz, the homeland of King George III's wife, Queen Charlotte. (I smile when I wonder if those early colonial plantation owners had any idea that the namesake of Charlotte and Mecklenburg Counties is said to have been of African and Moorish descent.)

Chase City, when it was known as Christiansville, was settled by the king's colonists from other regions of Virginia as well as from Pennsylvania and Maryland. The slaveholding Elam family of

Mecklenburg County traces its heritage back through the generations to Brodsworth Parish, Yorkshire, England, in the 1500s. Martin Elam, born in England in 1635, married Frances Perrin in 1675 in Henrico County, Virginia. One of Martin Elam's grandsons, Joel Elam, owned seventy-one acres on the upper middle section of Bluestone Creek, which flows into the Roanoke River. The Elams would later add additional land at Buffalo Springs, south of the Roanoke River, which flows into North Carolina.

Property and estate records and wills from the antebellum era as well as census records for the Reconstruction years following the Civil War list many slaves and former slaves identified with the Elam family name. The 1870 census for Bluestone Township lists fifteen Elam family members identified as black or mulatto, including children, farmhands, and housekeepers.

Tobacco made Mecklenburg County, where the rolling hills of the Piedmont settle into the Tidewater, one of the wealthiest counties in the Virginia commonwealth. The Prestwould plantation in Clarksville and the 1790s Boyd Tavern in Boydton remain popular tourist stops. South Hill offers the Tobacco Farm Life Museum of Virginia, with its focus on the family farm heritage of 1935–50, not the legacy of the slave economy of the Old South.

When I was in my midtwenties or early thirties, I joined my brothers Harry and Clarence to travel south to Chase City for an Elam family reunion. As we drove around, we saw a sign reading "Elam Jewelry Store," so we went in. My brothers and I talked to the owners, who sure didn't look like us, but they were gracious. I got up the nerve to say we could be related, and they responded, "We certainly could be." That was a pleasant surprise. It helped me move away from my built-in prejudices about white people with southern accents. It was a good thing for me to experience, and a good lesson for someone who did not want to go below the Mason-Dixon line.

My grandfather on my mother's side, Sherman Justin Lee, was from Aiken, South Carolina, but the names of his parents as well as the place and date of his birth are not known. The same is true for my grandmother on my mother's side, Henrietta Frazier Lee. She died in 1926, long before my birth, when my brother Harry Justin Elam was only about four years old. Yet he would later recall looking up at his grandmother's casket in the parlor of the family home at 194 Western Avenue, Cambridge, Massachusetts, as family and friends gathered in the days just before her burial. He writes that the word other family members would use in describing her was "regal," despite blindness late in life and the loss of one leg, amputated as the result of diabetes.

Grandpa Lee earned a living as a chauffeur for a well-to-do Brookline family. When he wasn't driving their family someplace, he was busy polishing the big black limousine in his driveway. He seemed to take great pride in always keeping the vehicle in tip-top condition. Grandpa Lee was the breadwinner, but our grandmother was "the principal person of authority in the Lee household whom everyone held in high regard," Harry wrote in his history of the family.

Their decision to leave South Carolina to resettle in Cambridge was a familiar one for many African American families of that era.

South Carolina, especially Aiken County and Edgefield County on its northern border, was not a safe place to raise a family in the early 1900s. It had not been a safe place for generations. There are some places where it is still not safe. During the writing of this book, a twenty-one-year-old hate-filled white man intending to start a race war shot and killed the pastor and eight members of the historic Charleston Emanuel African Methodist Episcopal Church in Charleston, South Carolina. At the man's first court appearance, surviving family members, in an act of faith and following their Christian tradition, expressed forgiveness to the man who had taken the lives of their relatives. Their powerful, heartbreaking message prompted South Carolina lawmakers to remove the Confederate battle flag from the grounds of the state capital.

Aiken County is South Carolina's only county created during Reconstruction. Neighboring Edgefield County's legacy is one of violence. The county often is singled out as one of the most savage counties in the South. The Edgefield District, which later became Edgefield and Aiken Counties, "was the 10th wealthiest county in the nation in 1850 and a jurisdiction known for hot-blooded adventurers such as William Travis, the martyred leader of the Alamo," reporter Jim Nesbitt wrote in a February 6, 2004, article for the *Augusta Chronicle*, "A Story Left Untold." The two counties are across the Savannah River from Augusta, Georgia. Edgefield also would be a "seat of power for ardent secessionists such as Gov. Francis Pickens," Nesbitt wrote.

As South Carolina's governor, Pickens "helped to ignite the Civil War by ordering his militia to seize federal property in Charleston," according to Fox Butterfield in his generational study *All God's Children: The Bosket Family and the American Tradition of Violence.*

In the decades of the South's slave economy before the Civil War, South Carolina's politics were solidly in the control of an entrenched landed aristocracy modeled after the elite of England's landed gentry. "Nowhere else in America did the wealthy class so successfully conspire to keep power away from the common man," writes William W. Freehling in his 1965 book *Prelude to Civil War.*

Founded on December 19, 1835, the city of Aiken was named after Irish immigrant William Aiken, the president of the South Carolina Canal and Railroad, who died in 1831 at his Charleston home. His railroad was founded in 1827 at his King Street house, now a historical site. His son, William Aiken Jr., would become the state's governor, serving from 1844 to 1846. He also served in the state legislature and the U.S. Congress, running unsuccessfully for Speaker of the House in 1856.

The western terminus of the rail line to the Savannah River was at Hamburg, South Carolina, linking the upcountry cotton plantations with the port and markets at Charleston. Hamburg had been founded in 1821 by Henry Schultz, a German immigrant who had a black wife.

Some sixty thousand bales of cotton a year were shipped out of Hamburg by rail in the 1830s and 1840s. However, expanded rail lines through the region in the 1850s made Hamburg a ghost town in the years before the Civil War. Hamburg became a haven for freedmen after the war.

Southerners would begin to describe the war as their "Lost Cause." Sherman's "March to the Sea" snaked through Aiken County. Slaves fled plantations to follow Sherman's army, and white families faced hard times. With the war's end, the defeated Confederacy saw "the bottom rail was put on top," as one bankrupted and politically marginalized planter's family worded it. Freedmen gained the vote, a right denied many poor whites. Black suffrage helped "Radical Republicans" take over state and local government. Congress revoked Sherman's promise of forty acres and a mule for freedmen, but Grant's Freedmen's Bureau set up schools and helped former slaves negotiate farm leases and sharecropping and labor contracts. Aiken's cotton yield topped Edgefield's.

A leading member of the Lee family was one of the founders of Aiken County. A courthouse stone-and-bronze marker celebrating Aiken County's 125th anniversary lists the name Samuel J. Lee, a freedman who owned a farm outside of Hamburg. Lee (1827–95) was born a slave on the cotton plantation of his father, Samuel McGowan of Abbeville County, upriver from what once was the Edgefield District. McGowan, a Confederate general, took along his mulatto son as his servant during the war. Wounded twice as a Confederate soldier, Lee later became a leader of a black militia unit during the federal occupation of the South. He won election to the state legislature, serving as the first black Speaker of the House. He would be the first black man admitted to the South Carolina bar.

Aiken County historian Owen Clary, in the Nesbitt article, points to "spite" as the key motivation to create the county. Radical Republicans decided to punish Edgefield County by slicing off a new Aiken County, where black voters would be in the majority.

Isabel Vandervelde writes in her book *Aiken County: The Only South Carolina County Founded during Reconstruction* that on March 10, 1871, Samuel J. Lee was one of three black lawmakers who led a state legislature dominated by blacks and Radical Republicans to create Aiken County. Lee is shown in a framed picture at the Aiken County Historical Museum's display of three black cofounders.

According to reporter Jim Nesbitt, "At the height of his power, he [Lee] was a state legislator, county commissioner, county registrar, and adjutant general in the black militia headquartered in Hamburg. He later served as county coroner and justice of the peace."

Freedmen faced violence from former Confederates and out-of-power southern Democrats, which marred South Carolina politics during the Reconstruction Era. Seven men, six black militiamen or civilians and a white farmer, were killed in a riot on July 8, 1876. The Hamburg Massacre erupted a few days after two white farmers from Edgefield County found the road through Hamburg blocked by a black militia military exercise of the South Carolina National Guard. Racial tension sparked hundreds of armed white men to confront some forty militiamen and Hamburg residents at an armory. Some of the townspeople died in battle; others were captured and executed by the white mob. The mob fired upon those who fled. White Democrats would use the Hamburg Massacre in their 1876 "Redemption" campaign to force Republicans out of office and end Reconstruction in South Carolina. The elections restored Democrats and white supremacist rule that ensured the next century of Jim Crow laws, crafted to deny civil rights for freedmen and their descendants.

With the end of Reconstruction, southern Democrats by 1878 had forced out black lawmakers with false charges of corruption. Samuel J. Lee's reputation survived the charges, and he moved to Charleston, where he became a prominent lawyer. When he died in 1895, his obituary ran in the *New York Times*. His white contemporaries considered Lee "one of the best criminal lawyers the State had produced. At his death all local courts were declared adjourned and the entire city paid him homage," writes Norman P. Andrews in his article "The Negro in Politics," published October 1, 1920, in the *Journal of Negro History*.

Family legend says the Lee family left South Carolina to resettle in Cambridge, Massachusetts, because Grandpa Lee was being harassed for printing and distributing literature condemning segregation and discrimination.

My maternal grandparents, Sherman Justin Lee and Henrietta Frazier Lee, raised five boys and two girls. My mother, Blanche Delnora Lee, was the one who had to give up school in the eighth grade to help her mother run the household when her mother became ill. She had five brothers in her care.

Ralph, the oldest, served in the army infantry during World War I. He later became an entertainer. As a member of the cast of a hit Broadway musical of the 1920s, *Shuffle Along* (written and directed by Noble Sissle and Eubie Blake), Ralph became known as "Bobby Lee, the Shuffler." "It seems he was originally a member of the male chorus and dance group. Once, as the chorus was exiting the stage, he accidentally stumbled but quickly recovered and did a bit of a strut as he was the last one to leave the stage. It no doubt caught the audience's attention for loud laughter erupted along with a spontaneous burst of applause. It seemed the audience really liked that strut Bobby Lee had improvised to cover up his stumble. It caught the attention of Sissle and Blake, who gave Ralph a solo role in the show doing his special dance called 'The Strut.'"

The second oldest, Herman Justin Lee, also a World War I vet, worked in the postal service. Fred, perhaps the most popular of the clan, was a jovial chap whom everyone liked to be around. He became a doorman at the New England Deaconess Hospital until his early death from tuberculosis. Willard, bedridden most of the time, is remembered for his smile, despite his illness.

Helen studied typing and shorthand in high school and found employment as the secretary to the first executive director of the Boston branch of the Urban League, George Goodman. Helen is credited with doing much of the work of the Urban League and finding decent jobs for blacks during the Depression years. For example, my brother Harry recalled that Helen helped the Morris family after they came up from Mobile, Alabama, in the early 1930s, a mother and father with six sons and three daughters. Each would have distinguished careers in Boston and beyond. The oldest of the Morris daughters praised Helen's advice and support. Harry added, "Aunt Helen gave all of her nieces and nephews great encouragement and support, pushing all of us to get a good education." She married late in life and died a short time later from diabetes.

Wyman, the youngest son, was an outstanding athlete in high school and played baseball in the Negro Leagues, when even the best of the black ballplayers were banned from the Major League. Wyman was a catcher and once caught for the inimitable Satchel Paige.

Wyman never played in the Major League. Like so many others in my family, his talents were veiled by a segregated America. When I began writing this memoir, I knew I needed to honor my family's legacy and lift that veil.

2

My Name Is Harriet

It is my will to found and endow an institution to be called Simmons Female College, for the purpose of teaching medicine, music, drawing, design, art, science, and industry best calculated to enable the scholars to acquire an independent livelihood. —JOHN SIMMONS, 1867

I was a very shy adolescent and teenager, often referred to as "the little Elam girl." No one seemed to know my first name. My sister and brothers were known quantities, but I was thought of as "the surprise" because I arrived almost seventeen years after my sister, who had been the baby and only girl until that time. My brothers were eighteen, nineteen, and twenty years older. I kept my parents young.

One day I mustered enough nerve to tell a church member who always called me "the little Elam girl," "My name is Harriet. I *have* a first name."

I was born in Boston, but all of my siblings were born in Cambridge.

My father was sixteen in 1907 when he moved from his birthplace in Virginia to Pittsburgh, Pennsylvania, to work in the steel mills. He lived with two brothers, John and Walter. In 1918 he joined the segregated army and served with a field artillery unit in France during World War I. After the war, he decided to look for work in Cambridge, Massachusetts.

In the spring of 1920, after meeting my mother on a blind date, my father proposed. The connection must have been very strong, for mother did not want to delay the wedding to wait for her only sister to finish teaching at a school in North Carolina, the Palmer Memorial

Institute. June was just too far away; so on March 10, 1920, Blanche Delnora Lee married Robert Harry Elam in the Lee family home on Worcester Street. It must have been quite a party, because a portion of the house's floor caved in during the reception.

When my parents passed away a few months apart in 1974, they had been married for fifty-four years. My mother, married to my father for all those years, was the consummate diplomat, fully aware that, while she might be right most of the time, she did not have to insist.

Born and reared in the South at a time when African Americans had few opportunities to obtain much in the way of a formal education, my parents nevertheless were an astute and resourceful pair, never despairing over the difficult circumstances they faced. When I reflect on their experiences, I am amazed that my parents raised five children who made them proud. With my dad's annual salary never more than $3,500, he was adamantly against welfare. It didn't matter what he did, he was going to make an honest living. That commitment is evident in all of his children. My mother was an unflappable soul, one who would never yield to adversity. She unabashedly performed day work in the homes of affluent white families to supplement the family income during the dark days of the Great Depression.

Dad became an auto mechanic, a trade he picked up after leaving the army. He opened his own repair shop on Soden Street in Cambridge, close to the Lee home on Western Avenue. In those days of segregated neighborhoods, black entrepreneurship could thrive. His business was beginning to do well during the late twenties, so he decided to expand his operation. An ideal location became available at the intersection of Western Avenue and Memorial Drive, which runs along the Charles River. No sooner had my father arranged the financing for the new venture and installed new equipment when along came the catastrophe of catastrophes, the Wall Street crash of 1929, followed by the Great Depression. My father lost everything: his new business, his equipment, and all of his tools. The only thing he managed to hold on to was a 1926 Hudson that he had repaired. The owner was unable to pay for the repairs, so Dad enforced his mechanic's lien.

With work hard to find for a man with a fifth-grade education, Dad found odd jobs to support his growing family. This was long before my birth, but as my brother Harry recalled in his papers about the family story, "My mother took in washing and worked as a domestic in the homes of doctors and other professionals in the Boston suburbs when she could find someone to care for the children. The family began to move around a lot, from the third floor of one three-decker apartment to another. We (there were four of us at the time, Charles, the oldest, was 8) did not understand why we had to move so many times in such a relatively short period of time."

The family lived in a series of three-bedroom apartments. The boys shared the same bed in one room. All attended Cambridge public schools. In 1932 the Elam family moved across the Charles River to the Roxbury section of Boston, another third floor of another three-decker, this one on Elbert Street, a dead-end street off Humboldt Avenue in the Sugar Hill section of Roxbury. At that time, Negro families lived on streets located on the lower end of Sugar Hill while Jewish families, then the predominant ethnic group in Roxbury, lived on the streets in the upper part of the hill. A public transportation trolley ran on tracks from Dudley Street in the lower end of Roxbury up Warren Street to Walnut Avenue, and then it continued up Humboldt Avenue to Seaver Street, which was at the top of the hill. Adjacent to Seaver Street is the spacious Franklin Park, a public area in the city containing the world-renowned Franklin Park Zoo.

Few families had automobiles. For a long time, the Elam family had the only car on the street. Many of the neighborhood families became lifelong friends. Harry recalled, "We played games together and accompanied each other on trips to the places where they dispensed free bread and milk and other rations to families who were victims of the Great Depression."

Roxbury is a very old Boston neighborhood. Puritans led by William Pynchon (1589–1661) settled there three weeks after the founding of Boston in 1630. They named it "Rocksberry" after bedrock outcroppings called Roxbury puddingstone. In the early to mid-1900s, African Americans living in the South End's Lower Roxbury moved into the Elm Hill-Sugar Hill neighborhood, replacing the Jewish community. Southern African Americans made their homes in Roxbury during and after World War II to work at nearby defense plants, including Raytheon in Newton. Martin Luther King Jr., while a theology student at Boston University, preached at the Twelfth Baptist Church on Warren Street in 1950.

The "Berry"—as Roxbury's black neighborhood was known then—also had been home to Malcolm Little as a teenager and young adult before he dropped his last name and began using an X. In his autobiography, Malcolm X described Roxbury's Dudley Square: "I didn't know the world contained as many Negroes as I saw thronging downtown Roxbury at night, especially on Saturdays. . . . Neon lights, nightclubs, pool halls, bars, the cars they drove! Restaurants made the streets smell—rich, greasy, down-home black cooking. Jukeboxes played Erskine Hawkins, Duke Ellington, Cootie Williams, dozens of others."

Despite the availability of the GI Bill, my oldest brother, Charles, did not want to go to college. Charles was, however, the one person we could rely upon in terms of keeping our homes well repaired, painted, and spotless. He worked for the Boston Transport Authority and was also a building superintendent who, like our dad, took pride in his work. Charles and his devoted wife, Alline, gave my parents seven grandchildren, all of whom made Blanche and Robert Elam proud. They remain centered in their faith and totally committed to improving the quality of life for those in need in their respective communities. The legacy of their deeply spiritual mother lives on today in their work.

The middle brother, Harry, became only the fourth African American judge on the Boston Municipal Court, the oldest trial court in the country. He became the chief justice of that court and later was appointed associate justice to the Massachusetts Superior Court. Harry practiced law with Edward Brooke in Boston, who would become the first popularly elected African American U.S. senator. My husband and I were delighted to accompany Harry to the U.S. Capitol October 28, 2010, when Senator Brooke, two days after the senator's ninetieth birthday, received from President Obama the Congressional Gold Medal, the highest civilian honor awarded by Congress. He and my brothers were friends for more than sixty years.

Senator Brooke was very much like a fourth brother to me. He recommended me for my first stateside job after my return from the embassy in Paris in 1968. (My life in Paris is covered in detail in a later chapter, as is the job the senator arranged for me on the transition team of incoming Republican president Richard Nixon. I would stay on as an appointments secretary for two years in the Nixon White House.)

My brothers pushed me to excel, and the senator was right there with them. He was always available when I needed counsel, particularly in preparation for my Senate confirmation hearing when I was named to be ambassador to Senegal, and he attended important ceremonies in my life, including my swearing in as ambassador. He called me in September 2014, as he always did on my birthday. I was in New York, so Wilfred spoke with him. I was honored to do a reading at his funeral at the National Cathedral on March 10, 2015. When he died at age ninety-five on January 3, 2015, at his home in Coral Gables, Florida, the *Washington Post* wrote that he was "one of only two African Americans to serve in the Senate in the 20th century. He was the first to serve since Reconstruction, when state legislatures appointed senators." A liberal Massachusetts Republican, Senator Brooke "was one of the most popular politicians in Massachusetts, known for his independence—from civil rights leaders and from conservative members of his party," the *Post* reported. The obituary continues, "He was a black, Protestant Republican representing a state that was more than 95 percent white, overwhelmingly Catholic and two-thirds Democratic. 'I do not intend to be a national leader of the Negro people. I intend to do my job as a senator from Massachusetts,' he told *Time* magazine after his Senate election."

The youngest of my brothers, Clarence, who died in 1985 while I was a cultural affairs officer in Athens, Greece, attended university under the GI Bill. He earned an undergraduate degree in business administration from Boston University and, much later, a law degree from

Suffolk University. He was the executive secretary of the Governor's Council during Christian Herter's term. Interestingly, Harry held the same position in another Massachusetts governor's administration.

Clarence was later appointed chairman of the Boston Licensing Commission. One of the key responsibilities of that job was to approve liquor licenses for hotels, restaurants, and bars. With the wisdom of age, I now know that the occasional case of wine or spirits from these grateful restaurant owners contributed to his alcohol dependency. However, many of the city hall employees genuinely respected Clarence because he made them feel important and valued. For the first time, I saw the positive results of supervisors treating staffers with respect. Clarence's approach taught me as much about management as the subsequent courses I took on the subject at the State Department. Clarence died of throat cancer. No doubt the alcohol exacerbated the throat cancer that led to his death.

The foundation of Clarence's friendship with Edward Brooke was the result of their service together during World War II in the all-black 366th Infantry in Italy. No doubt that mutual trust led to Clarence serving as one of Ed Brooke's key political advisors from Brooke's first campaigns in Massachusetts to his time in the U.S. Senate. Exposure to Italian life and culture created Clarence's love of Italian operatic composers. He frequently played opera and other classical music recordings, and I had no choice but to listen. When funds permitted, he would take me to concerts at Boston Symphony Hall. Let me be candid; I had minimal interest in such things at age fifteen and sixteen. However, I mellowed as I got older and wiser. I had no idea that a few decades later I would become a cultural attaché and host to some of America's most celebrated and respected performing artists of all musical genres during my diplomatic career. On many occasions, those artists prepared the ground for the United States to enter serious negotiations on a host of important international agreements. As I view the annual awards for the Kennedy Center Honors, I am thrilled to have been the host during my overseas assignments to many of these revered American artists.

Until his death, Clarence remained a part of Ed Brooke's inner circle. Clarence introduced Harry to Ed, and they became friends as well. In the mid-1950s Harry shared law offices with Brooke in Roxbury.

The Law Offices of Brooke and Elam became the community's resource for all things legal. They represented a majority of their clients pro bono. They served the community's legal needs and garnered unconditional support in their political ventures. Harry had an unsuccessful run for City Council but got the minority vote. Harry often said he became a judge because several leaders met with Governor Francis Sargent and said, "You need to make Harry Elam a judge." The governor took their advice, and Harry became, as I mentioned, a judge in the country's oldest trial court, the Boston Municipal Court.

Before my college years, I worked on local campaigns as a summer intern (although it was not called that at the time) at city hall and in my brother's law offices. In fact, for a long time I wanted to be a legal secretary. For some reason I was impressed with the blue covers on the summonses. That distinctive color automatically let the recipients know the legal document had consequences and they had better take action. To this day I am fascinated by legal proceedings.

My sister, Annetta Elam Capdeville, who was ninety when she died during the writing of this book, had endured Alzheimer's disease since she was sixty-five. She was my last remaining sibling. Once a gifted poet and writer, she remained the "soul" of the Elam family. My sister had a mellifluous voice. Before the early onset of her memory loss, she was writing the history of our family. Sadly, we have been unable to locate the original draft. Fortunately, Harry left us his writing on the family story, which provides a wealth of family history.

Clarence, Harry, and Charles were very close. My sister said my mother often asked her to take the blame for my brothers' pranks. My father was a harsh disciplinarian on the boys; yet he would not be harsh with Annetta. She bristled at my mother's requests but had little recourse. My mother said she could not bear to have those three young boys in the house on "detention" for a full week. The three brothers loved their little sister, no doubt, in part because she often saved them from harsh punishment. Once I arrived, my sister had to share the limelight with a new baby sister. It had to be very difficult.

As I mentioned, I was born in 1941, just a few months before the Japanese attack on Pearl Harbor prompted the United States to enter World War II. Harry describes my birth as "a most unexpected and yet most blessed event" for the Elam family. "Little did we know at the time how truly blessed an event this was; but in time, each and every member of our clan began to recognize and appreciate the special benediction we have been given."

Harry, then a sophomore in college in Virginia, clearly remembers the call from our mother, telling him he had a new baby sister.

> I asked, "What name have you given her?"
>
> "Harriet," she replied.
>
> And I said, "Oh, you missed me so much, you named her after me."
>
> My mother immediately responded. "No, I did not name her after you, I named her after Harriet Tubman."
>
> Boy, if my face could have turned red, it surely would have. Mom really put me in my place.

My parents passed away when I was only thirty-three. Yet until August 12, 2012, I was blessed to have an incredible surrogate father in my brother, Judge Harry Justin Elam. He had five children of his own, but he was the father figure in my life. He advised me through the many professional challenges in my diplomatic career and in graduate school. He gave me away when I married and swore me in in the historic Benjamin Franklin Room at the State Department when I became an ambassador.

By the time I was born, Dad was working as an automobile mechanic on large transport military vehicles at a Boston army base. My mother continued working as a domestic throughout my childhood. On several occasions I went to work with her using the well-known

Boston MTA. I enjoyed the bus and trolley ride as I viewed the elegant homes along the way. I remember reminding my mother, "Mama, you didn't do that corner." She would say, "I have four houses to do today; I didn't ask you to be my inspector. Just do what I asked that you do." One of the ladies would leave tea and crumpets or scones for us. I looked forward to going to that residence because this was one of the few ladies who demonstrated some humanity toward us. I have yet to see the film *The Help*, but I read Kathryn Stockett's book and decided I could not bear to watch the film. Too many of the incidents in the book reminded me of my mother. I might be overly sensitive to this point in my mother's life, but it is why I have been doubly careful about how I have interacted with every person on the char force at embassies, in the State Department, at UCF, or wherever I have encountered someone who ensures our workspace is clean and sanitary. I have one photo of my mother with two little white boys standing next to her. I do not know if she cared for them while raising my siblings. All I know is that she was "the help" as she cleaned the homes of Dr. Santoro and his sister, Lydia Gallassi.

When Harry was in the sixth grade at Henry Lee Higginson School on Harrishof Street, about four or five blocks from our home on Elbert Street, Roxbury was about equally split between Negro and Jewish neighbors. In the fall of 1933 he entered the seventh grade at Boston Latin School, which in 1635 became the future nation's first public school. Its alumni came from some of Boston's elite families. It stressed the classics with four years of Latin, beginning in the seventh grade. It is now located in the Fenway area, several miles northwest of Roxbury and across the street from Simmons College, near the city's major hospitals and Harvard Medical School. It remains one of the nation's top high schools and the city's premier school.

In the fall of 1940 Harry began his studies at Virginia State College in Petersburg. On his first trip into the South, he endured his first brush with Jim Crow. In Washington, he was directed to the rear of the train and the car designated for those then labeled "colored" people. Once in Petersburg, he was impressed with the historically black college's all-black faculty, many with advanced degrees. His history professor, Dr. Luther J. Jackson, was a voting-rights activist who traveled throughout the state, encouraging black citizens to pay the poll tax and elect candidates who would revoke the state-imposed tax.

Over his summer break, and anticipating that his draft notice would soon come, Harry worked as a red cap at the train station in Boston. War came, but because of his poor eyesight the draft board rejected him. Still hoping to enlist, he memorized the eye chart and won his enlistment at a different recruitment office. He trained for the signal corps, but the segregated army had no need for his skills. Instead, he was shipped off to the India-Burma border to dig holes and put up telephone poles. At the war's end and after his long liberty ship voyage back to Boston, his homecoming included his mother's fried chicken, mashed potatoes, collard greens, and sweet potato pie topped with Brigham's ice cream, still marketed as "Boston's Favorite Since 1914."

Harry expected his communications training in the army might bring him a job with the New England Telephone Company. He applied, but the phone company had no black employees before the war and the job opportunities were no better after the war.

Harry met his future wife, Barbara Aileen Clark, while singing in the church choir. She was sixteen and a freshman at Boston's Simmons College. Harry soon abandoned any plans to return to college in Virginia and enrolled at Boston University's College of Liberal Arts. After her graduation, Barbara and Harry married in 1949. He earned his law degree from Boston University soon afterward and joined the law practice of the future senator Ed Brooke.

When Harry began dating Barbara, I immediately fell in love with her almost as much as my brother did. Harry and Barbara, in a way, became my parents. A children's librarian who directed the Boston Public Schools Library Program, she introduced me to the joy of reading at a very early age. Barbara was one of the reasons I became interested in attending college. If I had become a legal secretary, I would have gone to a business or secretarial school. When I earned scholarships, one major one came from Simmons College. I was thrilled to go there because I loved Barbara so much that I wanted to be like her. Her influence on my life was significant. She was a voracious reader. As a result, she had worldly knowledge and an incredible vocabulary. In my preteen and teenage years, she would take me to museums, libraries, and children's concerts. To say I was a reluctant visitor was an understatement. I did not want to go, but once there, I became intrigued. Each time Harry and Barbara visited me abroad, she loved spending time in our Cultural Center American Libraries.

When I was about fourteen, my mother asked Barbara to be the sponsor and chaperone for a teenage club called the Teenettes. That interaction solidified my relationship with Barbara even more. My mother believed young ladies should know about proper etiquette, appropriate attire, and suitable comportment in social settings. In essence, we were to be exposed to the "finer things in life." My dear mother did not give my sister-in-law a chance to say no. We had teas, fashion shows, and inspirational speakers. We hosted Gloria Lockerman, the black student from Baltimore who was twelve years old in 1955 when she won the television program that predated *Jeopardy*, *The $64,000 Question*. Imagine a young television celebrity who was known for her academic ability visiting my home. We also met Tom Mboya, a Kenyan politician during Jomo Kenyatta's government. Clarence met Mboya during a 1968 visit to Africa with Senator Brooke. Mboya spearheaded negotiations for Kenya's independence from the British. He was assassinated in July 1969 in Nairobi.

My parents' attitude and experiences had a positive impact on all their children, particularly on me. Many of my friends' parents were divorced or separated. I grew up in a stable environment and attended the Boston Public Schools, which were at that time among the best in the nation. And, because my brothers were so much older, they were almost my fathers. A few weeks before I was scheduled to enter Lewis Junior High, which was known more for disciplinary problems than for its academic successes, Clarence and Harry went to Boston City Hall. They informed the responsible persons that their little sister should attend the more reputable Patrick T. Campbell Junior High. They succeeded in their request, and I was transferred to the Campbell school. I walked approximately five miles round trip each day. I was too frightened to use public transport to get to the new school, for I would have to transfer at the rough Dudley Station stop where scores of students congregated. I avoided Dudley Station during the after-school hours as much as I could. The walking helped my weight problem.

I cannot sing like my sister, but I memorized biblical passages in Sunday school and recited poems at church teas. Clearly, I wanted my parents' approval, so I began to develop enough nerve to speak in public. Perhaps that is why I speak almost too much now.

After I finished junior high, my parents enrolled me in Boston's classics-oriented high school for girls, Girls' Latin School (now the coed Boston Latin Academy). In 1878 it became the first college preparatory high school for girls when activist mothers lobbied for their daughters to gain admittance to the then all-male Boston Public Latin School. My parents thought that I should follow my brother Harry, who attended Boston Latin. I thought that was a fate worse than death. After four months I asked my parents to take me out of that school. I struggled with Latin and constantly reminded them I was not like my brothers. I did not wish to be like them. They took me out.

The guidance counselor at Roxbury Memorial High School for Girls first assigned me to the commercial course track. My brothers were again outraged. They visited that counselor and reminded her that my grades merited assignment to the academic track. Had it not been for my brothers' initiative, I would not have been enrolled in the academic track and may well not have entered college.

Only a few of the girls at my high school were black. Even though it was located in a predominantly black area, it was considered one of the most competitive all-girls schools after Girls' Latin. I enjoyed a diverse pool of friends at that time: Italian, Polish, and a few of Latino descent. For those of us who are left, we are as close now as we were then. The interaction between races even in Boston at that time was relatively positive. Our main goal was to be educated. I liked my classmates and had no preconceived notions about them because of their origins. Children have to be taught to hate.

Because I had such strict parents, I dared not step out of line in school. I probably deserved the nickname "Little Miss Goody Two Shoes." My social life at that stage in life was nonexistent. Overweight and very shy, I found refuge from society in my homework. Back then I wore size eighteen gym bloomers. That was really big. Consequently, I was not a sports enthusiast. Totally inept in social settings, I dared not speak to anyone I did not know. I was a wallflower. I followed the rule in those days that children were to be seen and not heard.

I lost weight during adolescence, and at sixteen, thanks to my sister-in-law June Elam's influence, I worked in Dr. Lewis's drugstore. I hand-packed ice cream and made root beer floats, banana splits, and hot fudge sundaes. I am sure I ate a few of those sundaes as well. This service-oriented job helped bring me out of my shell. I had to talk to people I did not know and had to be polite.

The first time I had a positive sense of myself is when I received three of my high school's college scholarships. At seventeen, I realized I did something right. Boston University and Simmons College were my top choices. I received acceptances from both. I chose Simmons because Barbara was an alumna, but also because Simmons was smaller and seemed to offer more individual attention. I knew I needed that. The interview process at Boston University was intimidating because of the number of students seated outside the interview rooms. Jane Curtin, Simmons's dean of admission, took an interest in me and responded to all of my questions.

The Simmons experience changed my life. I no longer had to compete with my brothers. My English professor, Dr. Charles L'Homme, my French professor, Dr. James Newman, and the dean of the School of Business, Woodrow Baldwin, took me under their wings. And Geraldine Morenski, another commuting student, became my closest college friend and remains my friend to this day. Friends who attended large universities often lamented that their professors did not present the material in an engaging fashion. The three individuals I just mentioned were masters at bringing the texts and grammar alive. These professors opened my eyes to worlds beyond the confines of Boston, and I was hooked.

At Simmons, I joined Delta Sigma Theta, founded in 1913 at Howard University and now the largest African American Greek-lettered sorority in the world. The oldest is Alpha Kappa Alpha. The worst part of pledging Delta was having to wear a baseball cap with "Bird Brain" emblazoned on the front! Now, for someone who thought she was pretty bright, spending six months being called "Bird Brain" was not fun. Of course, this was mild compared to some of the hazing going on today. It certainly worked on my psyche and helped me remain humble later in life.

My first visit to Howard University was to pin my dear friend Lynda Welch when she became a Delta, and that visit was an eye opener. I had never visited a historically black college or university. When I returned home, I told my mother, "Now I can understand somewhat why certain folk think we all look alike!" Honestly, I saw a sea of faces that looked like me and all were dressed to the nines. It was a vastly different sight from Simmons, where there were only four women of color. Truly, I had never before seen so many absolutely stunning women as I saw all over that campus, and they were so self-assured. I was impressed.

A month prior to the summer of my junior year, Mr. Baldwin, dean of the School of Business at Simmons, learned I had been accepted for the Experiment in International Living's Student Exchange Program. When he called to learn the status of my application, I confirmed I had been accepted, but I could not travel because I did not have the $1,100 to travel to France. Three days after that conversation, Mr. Baldwin's office called and informed me that a group of Boston businessmen in international affairs had provided me a $900 scholarship. I was ecstatic. Somehow my siblings, mainly my two brothers, Clarence and Harry, raised another $200, which covered the balance and a little extra for travel expenses, clothes, and the like. Trust me, $200 in 1962 was like $2,000 today. My summer in Lyon, France, truly gave me my first exposure to the world beyond the confines of the United States. The seed was planted.

Mme Marthe Sassard and her daughter Paule welcomed me into their home. They accepted me far more graciously than did many in my hometown of Boston. Throughout my young adulthood, I knew I had to prove myself. I had to be better than the rest. All of sudden to be accepted no matter what color was a defining moment. I thank my siblings and Simmons College for having given me that opportunity.

Until 1962, I tried to prove that I was academically equal to all of my white classmates. Consequently, I always tried to excel. I wanted to make my parents proud. In France I did not have to prove anything. This family welcomed me into their midst. For three months, I slept in the room where my French mother taught the cello. I shared the space with a baby grand piano and other musical instruments. They took me to classical music concerts and to historic sites in the area. I shall never forget when I witnessed my first symphonic orchestra performance of Debussy's *La Mer*. I was enthralled. It was as if a new window on my life had opened.

In 1962 few young black women lived in France and traveled to Switzerland and northern Spain. Few watched Bastille Day fireworks at Basilique de Fourvière in Lyon, France. Even fewer were fortunate to live in a town called Bron, a suburb about fifteen minutes from downtown Lyon. I actually rode bicycles, camped out, and visited the ruins of World War II. I had never done such things in Roxbury. The French students were far better informed about international events than most of my group of ten American exchange students.

The most positive memory I have of that summer was hearing a passer-by say, "La jeune noire, comme elle est belle!" (The young black one, how pretty she is!) Other than my parents, no one had ever described me as pretty. For a stranger to make that observation, I was flabbergasted. Trust me; I do not suffer from false illusions. I have looked at myself in the mirror for more than seven decades, and I am well aware beauty pageants were not in my destiny. However, just hearing that phrase lifted my soul.

Paule Sassard visited my family in Boston the following summer. The city of Boston was so welcoming of this exchange student from France that I got to visit the mayor's office and many of Boston's historic sights because Paule was my guest. I even went to Bunker Hill, which is in South Boston, an area where blacks were not welcomed in the mid-1960s.

While I was posted to Istanbul, Turkey, Paule, Mme Sassard, and Paule's son, Huge, (pronounced "you-gah") spent a week with me. Their 1992 visit allowed me to say a very special *merci beaucoup* for their welcome to me thirty years earlier. From classical concerts to museum visits and meetings with significant members of the arts community in Istanbul, I tried to match the hospitality they showed me when I was their guest many years earlier.

In September 2013 I spent my birthday with Paule Sassard-Serusclat, who had become a homeopathic doctor. Her late husband, Franck Serusclat, had been a French senator from Lyon. One of the staff aides gave us a private tour of the elegant chambers, meeting rooms, and libraries of the Senate, located on the historic grounds of the Palais du Luxembourg. What a thrill to be guided through the majestic settings and to have lunch in the senate dining room. A relationship formed in 1962 had led to this lifelong friendship.

That first summer living in France convinced me that I could change perceptions of America's minorities. Although it certainly was not a conscious effort, my mere presence in a group of ten American students delivered a message that no television program could deliver. I was "different" from the general perception of Americans. I was black, I spoke French, and I was (at least I thought) well educated. I believed I was the embodiment of that "other," which most French had seen only in newsreels or situation comedies.

During my senior year at Simmons, I relished memories of my French family's unconditional acceptance. That was not always the case when I was home in Boston. Gerry Morenski was my closest classmate. Our families sat together at a graduation dinner. Gerry's mother and my parents got along wonderfully. It was her older aunt Ruth, described by Gerry as a "very judgmental woman who was used to getting her own way," who objected when she learned she would be sitting with the Elam family. As Gerry tells the story, her mother agreed that the aunt was being ridiculous and also agreed to tell the aunt she could stay home if she objected. Gerry's uncle had met my father at a father-daughter event, and he made it known to Gerry he was absolutely thrilled to come to the dinner. On the way home, he pulled off to the Mass General exit on Storrow Drive. Gerry's family had listened to the aunt yap on and on about what a lovely evening we had shared. Her uncle had been silent. But once he stopped the car, he talked. He pointed his finger at his wife and said, "Do not talk." He then turned to Gerry in the backseat of his car. He very emotionally thanked her for doing the right thing, and he thanked Gerry's mother for "raising her right." He said that if it was not for Gerry they would have missed out on a wonderful evening with wonderful people. Gerry and her mother were stunned. The uncle never spoke up to his wife, and he was obviously very intent on making sure that she understood just how wrong she had been. Amazingly, from that night on, Aunt Ruth softened up. She was always truly interested in hearing about my career and world travels. Gerry's daughter, Kathleen Morenski, has been a career diplomat for twenty years and credits me for that inspiration. Kathleen, now fifty, established a study abroad scholarship in my name for students of international affairs at Simmons.

3

Do You Know How to Type?

When you're posted abroad, I guarantee that some of your foreign colleagues will know more than you about American history, and they'll know more than you about international relations theory and the structures of international affairs. . . . They will have studied American history—and lots of it. And you? You don't want to get hosed by your foreign counterparts. —JACK ZETKULIC, executive director of the Association for Diplomatic Studies and Training, 2005

During the summer prior to my senior year in high school, my mother insisted that I learn typing and shorthand. I did not want to attend any summer school for fear of giving the impression that I needed to improve my grades. After all, I was a fine student, and the last thing I needed was to diminish my academic accomplishments. Turns out, yet again, she was right.

In the early 1960s when women graduated from liberal arts colleges, often the first question visiting U.S. government recruiters posed was, "Do you know how to type?" After I graduated from Simmons with a degree in international business, a Department of Army recruiter asked the same question, and I said, "Yes, I know how to type." My family in Boston would have helped me find a job close to home, but there I would always be my siblings' little sister. Instead, I took a job in Washington as a secretary in the Department of the Army.

That year in DC was less than exciting. My work was routine and absolutely boring. I lived in the home of Mrs. Ruth Johnson, originally from Malden, Massachusetts. She was the great-aunt of my sorority sister from Boston, Kathy Stewart. I paid fifteen dollars a week for a lovely room in her home at 67 Gallatin Street nw. My room was newly painted and attractively furnished with a single bed, a blue and white flowered bedspread, and one of those old-fashioned dressing tables with mirrors. When my folks visited Aunt Ruth's home, which she owned by the way, they were very pleased. Aunt Ruth was one of the elevator operators at the State Department. She wore a stunning navy blue uniform with a white lace handkerchief in her pocket each day. I loved hearing her stories of the elegant diplomatic receptions when Angier Biddle Duke was the chief of protocol. These were the days before elevators were automated, and one of these lovely ladies controlled every elevator in the main State Department building. Today we rarely see these ladies unless there is a swearing-in ceremony or special events in the diplomatic rooms on the eighth floor of the department. I have been told three or four are still on the staff.

My parents were relieved that I was going to be in the home of a fine upstanding woman from Boston. They were ecstatic. I cannot say I shared their enthusiasm, but I was blessed to have been in such a welcoming environment. There was one major problem from my perspective. I was twenty-one and wanted to be independent. Living with Aunt Ruth was almost like living at home. One night I did not get home from work until 9:00 p.m., for I had gone to dinner with some of the other young women in the office. As I entered her home, Aunt Ruth was sitting in the living room. Clearly concerned, she wanted to know where I had been. I did not dare to show my frustration, although I was tempted. After explaining to her where I had been, I decided I would alert her to a possible late night out in advance. After it was clear I had no idea how to cook, Aunt Ruth offered to prepare my dinners if I gave her five dollars more a week. I did, and my life could not have been better. Despite the absence of total independence, I was working in the nation's capital, surrounded by museums, theaters, the Kennedy Center, and the Arena Stage. During the summer Aunt Ruth entertained many of her Boston relatives on her back patio, including my friend Kathy and her parents. The barbeque menus contained far more tasty foods than I had in Boston. I relished visits from Kathy's grandmother and

Aunt Ruth's sister, Esther Humphrey. Perhaps because I spent much time with my mother's friends, I always felt more comfortable with those older than I.

I joined Aunt Ruth's church, Peoples Congregational Church, and I remained a member of that church until I came to Orlando in 2003. My husband and I were married in that church.

After working a year in Washington, I accepted a two-year assignment overseas as a secretary in the political section of the American embassy in Paris. This second experience in France gave me an even broader view than I had in my controlled adolescence. My parents would never have allowed me to go to a nightclub. I never even went to a bar when I was at Simmons College.

In August 1965, very soon after I arrived in Paris, I saw this tall, elegant woman of color walking through the embassy. She was a Foreign Service secretary, but I thought she must be the head of the Economic Section because of the way she carried herself. She seemed to command whatever space she entered, and the stunning halls of the embassy in Paris added to her already arresting presence. After introductions, Mary Pearl Dougherty invited me to her home. She had a flat in Neuilly-sur-Seine. My apartment was in the same western suburb of Paris. During our first conversation, I learned she knew some of the same people in Boston my parents knew. Well, that was almost a marriage made in heaven. I'd been in France less than a week and I was so homesick. I could not wait to call my mother and father to tell them I met a women who knew Mrs. Boles, the wife of Boston's top black architect, Henry Boles. Mary Dougherty also knew Enoch Woodhouse, a Boston lawyer, community activist, and one of the famed Tuskegee airmen. Again my parents and I celebrated the fact that I had met someone with a strong Boston connection.

Mary Pearl Dougherty, who was eighty-eight when she died in Washington in 2003, was often called "the black Perle Mesta." Perle Mesta was known as the hostess with the "mostest" because of her elegant parties at her posts abroad and in Washington. Mary, too, was a gifted hostess. Her postings during a thirty-year career took her to Liberia, South Vietnam, the Central African Republic, Zaire,

Germany, and Romania. She was a secretary at the embassy, but for me and many other young black Foreign Service officers, Mary was a surrogate mother with an ease in giving advice on everything from how to deal with being overseas and away from family during holidays to the right glasses to use at dinner parties to serve cognac and cocktails, especially the layered colors of pousse-café. (Many years would pass before my refined husband would enjoy his Rémy Martin VSOP in his special cognac glass.)

Before coming to Paris, Mary Dougherty had worked for Dr. Carter G. Woodson, the "Father of Black History Month," who took on a scholarly crusade to document African American life and history. In her way, Mary carried on Woodson's work, "adopting" young Foreign Service staff and guiding their careers.

I had expected to be ready to go home after my first year in Paris, but, under Mary's tutelage, I ended up staying three years. She took me to the American Church in Paris and the American Cathedral. She introduced me to several American military officers and their families. She introduced me to a number of the important people of all hues at the embassy. If I thought my life had changed from the exchange experience in Lyons, the entrance of Mary Dougherty into my life made the Lyon summer pale in comparison. With Mary as my mentor for the next thirty years, I became a more self-assured adult, and eventually a full-fledged career diplomat.

As time went on, Mary introduced me to a world more sophisticated than any I knew in Boston. I learned how to eat artichokes, mushrooms, and other international delicacies. I actually attended jazz clubs after midnight. I accompanied her to plays where the language was rather spicy. I was twenty-three years old, away from the cocoon of Boston, and living in Paris. One play, *The Dutchman* by LeRoi Jones, later known as Amiri Baraka, had one reference that was rather base. I turned to Mary with a puzzled look and asked what the phrase meant. "Do you really want me to explain?" she said. By her look, I knew, no, no. It's okay.

Throughout my Paris assignment, my mother bought my clothes from the renowned Filene's Basement discount store in Boston. Once,

Mary knew I had been invited to an elegant cocktail event. She told me I needed what we called a basic, evergreen cocktail dress. I spotted this stunning red designer dress in the window of a shop along Faubourg Saint-Honoré, one of Paris's chic streets. Mary was with me. She walked with me into the store and ordered me to try it on. She then said, "You have to buy that. I will pay for it with my American Express, and you can pay me back." Buying a dress with a credit card was totally foreign to me at the time. Besides, it was $250. I could not buy a dress for that kind of money. I was making about $4,300 a year. Mary purchased the dress, and I wore it to many of the cocktails and receptions I attended for the next three years.

In Mary's little Volkswagen bug, we traveled around the wine country of France and Germany with her dear friend Alice Lee, who often called me "Peck's Bad Girl," from the 1959 television sitcom.

During my time in Paris, the Vietnam peace talks were underway. I could not believe the delay in those talks because the participants could not decide on the shape of the negotiating table. There were anti–Vietnam War demonstrations in front of the embassy. I must admit, it was frightening to observe hundreds of people swarming the streets in front of the embassy before the post-9/11 barriers and concrete blocks were installed. I was impressed by watching the elite French riot force, Compagnies Républicaines de Sécurité (State Security Police Force), appear seemingly from nowhere and move hundreds of demonstrators with such precision from the embassy perimeter. The riot squad never seemed to use force nor tear gas but succeeded in moving the frequent demonstrators.

The Left Bank of Paris experienced student unrest during the mid-1960s similar to the unrest during the civil rights movement in America. While the objectives were different, the actions were similar. Undaunted by the unrest, Mary would drive to the Left Bank. The tires of her little car would hit loose cobblestones that students had thrown in the streets. Nobody threw stones at us, but the streets were littered with stones. She wanted me to see the demonstrations. I think she wanted to sensitize me to what American student activists were doing back home. She figured I had plenty of book knowledge, but I was far from streetwise. She, like my mother regarding the typing and shorthand skills, was absolutely right about my naïveté.

Here I was in Paris during the height of the civil rights movement, 1965–68. I have mixed feelings about my absence from the States during the nonviolent demonstrations that have allowed me and so many others to hold the positions we hold today. Despite not being home at this critical time in U.S. history, I might well have made a positive contribution. I was "different." Honestly, if anyone said to me one more time during those years, "but you are not like the others," I would have screamed. My French was more fluent than that of my white counterparts in that section of the embassy. These colleagues wanted me to go with them wherever they went on weekends. For those three years, I was their "friend" because I was their interpreter.

Many of the French citizens I met were genuinely curious about the life of Negroes in America. I was one of the few American Negroes they had met who communicated in their language. It is my hope that I might have helped change their misperceptions of America. Most of my French friends were curious about my family. Whenever I described my parents' humble beginnings and my siblings' accomplishments, they became even more intrigued. I merely stated facts about the Elam family in Boston. After these "reality checks," I think many of the young French men and women I encountered revised the stereotypical images they had about American Negroes from print and television media.

Thus began my journey to bridging cultural divides. Although representing America was not my official duty, I began to make it my personal goal to let others know that there are many African Americans who are well read and educated, speak multiple languages, and communicate effectively across cultures. As I advanced to middle and senior levels in my diplomatic career, I realized that every action I took often impacted the views of my host country colleagues about the United States.

Even though I was away from the United States at the height of the civil rights movement, I kept abreast of everything that transpired in my hometown of Boston. On April 4, 1968, as I drove up the

Champs Élysée toward my studio apartment in Neuilly, I learned of Dr. King's assassination. I pulled off on Avenue Victor Hugo, parked the car, cried, and sat mesmerized as I listened to the news. In the days to come, I found out my hometown of Roxbury was also in the news, for the black population, devastated by King's assassination, reacted as those living in many other large urban areas reacted. I read in *Time* magazine how the mayor of Boston, with my brother, Judge Harry Elam, drove through the streets to calm the crowds and managed to minimize the damage that would have been incurred had riots broken out. In essence, I had not lost touch, for my family kept me informed of all that transpired during that difficult period in America's history. How blessed I was to have met Dr. King when he came to speak at the American Church in Paris.

After another Sunday service at the American Church in Paris, Mary Pearl Dougherty and I saw a young woman listening to the organ postlude in the back of the church. Born in New Jersey, of African American and German descent, jazz organist Rhoda Scott had come to Paris to study under a well-known classic organist and teacher, Nadia Boulanger. Not many people sit in the back of a church and listen to a classical piece as she did. We engaged in conversation, and the next thing we knew Mary invited both of us to her home the following weekend to help prepare a dinner. Mary threatened to leave Rhoda and me alone in her flat to prepare dinner. Neither Rhoda nor I had any idea of how to prepare artichokes, much less ratatouille (ra-ta-too-eeh). We were near panic until Mary relented and agreed to teach her novice chefs. Near the end of our vegetable preparations, Mary asked Rhoda to make lemonade. Rhoda asked if I could help her make the lemonade. I thought, how naïve, but I helped her make lemonade. Later in the evening, Mary and I went with Rhoda to the Left Bank Club Saint-Germain-des-Prés. Rhoda, the featured artist, was playing the organ. When she finished her set, I jokingly said, "If you want a recipe for a glass of water, I will gladly find one for you." Rhoda was a master of the organ. A friendship of forty-five years began, and Rhoda played at my seventieth birthday party in 2011.

Rhoda has performed at the Newark Jazz Festival, the Lincoln Center, the Kennedy Center, and Carnegie Hall for the Newport Jazz Festival after its move to New York. On the West Coast, she has performed at the Monterey Jazz Festival and at the San Francisco Jazz Festival. Yet Rhoda is another example of artists of color who have earned more recognition overseas than in their own country. The French love her. She's an icon in France. Rhoda has been honored by the French government as a *commandeur*, the highest grade of its Ordre des Arts et des Lettres. In 2014 she received her second master's in music with honors from Rutgers University.

In July 2007 Paule Sassard-Serusclat, my close friend from France, met me in the charming town of Nuits St. Georges to celebrate Rhoda's birthday. Rhoda gave yet another of her stellar performances. I was thrilled to share this experience with Paule, who had known Rhoda by reputation but had not met her.

Mary Dougherty continued my education by introducing me to another respected woman of color. Dr. Margaret Just Butcher, the oldest daughter of Dr. Earnest Just, a famed cell biologist, was probably the most erudite person I ever knew. She must have been in her fifties when I met her. I was twenty-three, perhaps twenty-four. This woman was a political appointee, but as the assistant cultural attaché in the American embassy in Paris in about 1966, she was revered by all of the artists and writers in Paris. She held one of the most coveted cultural assignments in Paris. She was respected because of her literary prowess. For me, it was mind boggling to be in the presence of this African American woman who had been a Fulbright scholar and was noted in our history for her work with the writer, philosopher, and educator Alain Locke, the first African American Rhodes scholar. Known for his promotion of black art and culture, Locke is recognized as the dean of the Harlem Renaissance. Just before he died in 1954, he had been working on his greatest work. He trusted the bright daughter of a close friend with his research, and Margaret took on the task of completing Locke's *The Negro in American Culture*, a reference book on African American contributions to American culture.

One of Margaret Butcher's contemporaries, Gerri Major, was a longtime senior staff editor for *Ebony* magazine and society editor for *Jet* magazine, writing from Paris. There were enough African Americans living and visiting in Paris at the time that *Ebony* thought it was worth opening an office in Paris, its first overseas bureau. Charles Saunders was the director. He collaborated with Gerri for their weekly Paris-focused society column. Writ large and holding their places in the academic realm, Gerri and Margaret reminded me of pictures you see of the grande dames of culture, seated in velvet chairs and holding walking sticks. They exhibited a certain gravitas that only they could because of their life experiences and knowledge of American literature and the arts. Both of them liked to drink cognac. As Saunders was preparing to leave Paris, he noted in his column that an admirer had just sent a case of Rémy Martin VSOP to Gerri's apartment overlooking the Avenue des Champs-Élysées. Gerri and Margaret would sit with their little glasses of cognac and hold court at Dr. Butcher's apartment on the Left Bank. Never once did I see them intoxicated, but when I took one sip of the stuff I thought, "Oh, my heavens, this is really strong stuff." This sheltered kid from Boston was in a whole new world.

When *Ebony* held a reception for the opening of its office on rue Georges V, all the elite of Paris, black and white, cultural icons and theatrical artists, attended. Once again I was enthralled to be in the presence of these writers and artists. There were lots of references to James Baldwin, Richard Wright, and other Negro artists who had been welcomed in Paris. Many African American writers were part of that expatriate renaissance. They were able to live and create with respectability and pride outside the United States. It was an eye-opening time for me in ways I had never imagined back in Boston. In 2013, on a return visit to France, I took the opportunity to join Ricki Stevenson's Black Paris Tour. This Stanford grad with a master's in history had been a television network news anchor-reporter who later spent six years as an international travel reporter. Her Paris tour is well documented and filled with history. It certainly opened my eyes to a wealth of information about black Americans who lived, worked, and created masterpieces while in the Paris of old. There is a brand new crop of artists and writers there today. As I remember those times in the 1960s, I'm listening to Mighty Mo Rodgers's "Black Paris Blues," in which he sings about the City of Light welcoming black artists, writers, and musicians. His song is a reminder of how music delivers messages that speeches and conferences do not.

Into that setting came my mother and father for a Paris visit in 1966. These two elderly black folk visited their youngest daughter for almost three weeks. My dad served in France during the First World War and was amazed to revisit sites he remembered. He recognized many of the buildings on the rue Royale. The French government insisted that historic façades could not be altered whenever interior renovations took place. Daddy beamed with joy to see them. We even took a trip to London. When we arrived in London, my geography and history lessons came alive. At the Tower of London, I saw the Beefeaters in their traditional uniforms. I saw the historic sites I had read about in school. Suddenly history became interesting. My teachers had told me history was relevant to our daily lives, but I wasn't really convinced until this trip. To see this senior couple viewing these scenes lifted my heart. Fortunately, my mother's journal from this trip still exists.

I planned a gathering in my Neuilly studio apartment to introduce my parents to my friends. My mother took one look at the invitation and said I should not use the words "cocktail party" on the invite. She said, "I am a deaconess at St. Mark Congregational Church. Deaconesses do not attend cocktail parties." (My father was never as much of a churchgoer as my mother. He would attend Easter and Christmas services.) I changed the wording on the invitations from a "cocktail party" to "a welcome gathering for my parents." I also had to hide a case of Scotch I had purchased, for I wasn't quite sure how my parents would feel about their daughter having that much alcohol in her residence. Forty-four guests attended. I quickly found out I had much more to learn about hosting a reception. I mixed every drink, as my father had done with his highballs at home. I put a cherry in every one of the drinks. One gent came into the kitchen and asked me to remove the cherry from his scotch and soda. With great embarrassment, I apologized and decided I would not put a cherry in every drink after that.

I had alerted Mary Dougherty that my parents were not likely to drink much alcohol because I had never seen my dad have a glass of wine. He only drank highballs, and that was usually on very special occasions. My mother would sip a bit of brandy, but she always told me it was for medicinal purposes. Much to my surprise, when asked, they told Mary they would "sample" her wine. They not only sampled the wine, they each drank a full glass. I was dumbfounded.

On another night, Mary took my parents to the Lido to see a show with scantily dressed women on stage. I was shocked because they seemed to enjoy the performance. Remember, these were the parents who gave me the impression that they were very straitlaced.

While in Paris, I met Olive and Everett Kelsey, a classy young Negro couple, thanks again to Mary Dougherty. Everett was one of the first young Negro bank officers on Chase Manhattan Bank's overseas staff. They had two toddlers, a real family unit. Seeing them warmed my heart, much the same way I am uplifted when I see the Obama children. Sadly, Everett died at the very young age of thirty-one, shortly after their return to the United States in 1968. Olive became a widow at age thirty-one. Her lovely daughter, Holly, a Middlebury College graduate, was killed in a car accident when she was only twenty-four, in 1981. Her son, Everett, resides in Los Angeles. Olive hosts me twice a year in her New York apartment when I attend the board meetings of the Institute of International Education. Despite the tragedies of her life, Olive is one of the most centered women I know. An avid reader of all things dealing with international affairs, literature, history, the arts, music, and sports, she is a captivating conversationalist An English teacher and museum executive, Olive taught English for two years in the Peoples' Republic of China. She continues to educate those fortunate enough to meet her. She has weathered life's challenges, never expresses bitterness, and continues to share her incredible knowledge with those smart enough to listen.

Until her passing in 2016, I stayed in touch with another friend from Paris, Virginia "Ginger" Cohen. While a professional colleague, Ginger was an unpretentious American jazz aficionado, artist, and jewelry creator. Ginger and Mary often took me to a place called the Living Room, between the Champs-Élysées and the Faubourg Saint-Honoré, where Art Simmons, an American pianist, played and collected much of the material for his Paris Sketchbook column for *Jet* magazine.

Pearl Richardson and Cecile "Cy" Richardson, both deceased (2012 and April 2015, respectively), were among my surrogate parents when I was truly "green behind the ears" in Paris. While I was unsophisticated in the ways of the world, they took me to exhibits and helped me adjust to life abroad. Pearl and Cy figure prominently in my becoming "finished."

With $750 from my income tax refund, I enrolled in a Paris finishing school. I learned how to walk and how to hold my purse, gloves, and a glass of champagne in my left hand while keeping my right hand free to greet people. I learned how to carry on conversations in international settings. I went to finishing school classes after work for five or six months. It was absolutely fun for me. I was there with all these razor-thin women who were trying to become models. But there were a few of us who just wanted to learn decorum and etiquette. Graduation included a formal dinner. We wore our long-sleeved gloves and gowns. The dinner table had more forks, spoons, and knives than one could ever imagine, but they prepared us for the experience of a formal sit-down dinner. Pearl and Cy enjoyed teasing me from time to time as they asked, "Harriet, are you finished yet?"

Pearl and Cy sat at the table with Virginia Cohen and Rhoda Scott at my seventieth birthday event in 2011. Much to my delight, they announced, "We think you're finished, Harriet!"

Another couple to welcome me to Paris, Jeannie and Gabriel Jacir, lived upstairs in the same Neuilly apartment complex where I resided. During a welcome dinner at their home, I ate the entire first course, thinking that was it. Three more courses followed. I dared not show my ignorance and sampled a bit of the remaining courses, all of which were delicious. I also learned about the intermezzo, when sorbet was served between courses to clear the palate.

Fortunately, I lived right downstairs. Aunt Ruth might not have been present in Paris, but the Jacirs certainly took her place. Whenever I came home from work in the spring or summer, I noted they were perched on their upstairs balcony to welcome me. If I ever thought I might have a romantic interest, I could depend on Jeanne and Gabriel being aware of the time the gent arrived and when he left. Did I say I thought I would find real independence when I moved to France?

I am not so sure I was "finished," but I was finished with Paris. Despite three wonderful years living and working in "the City of Light," the work was not challenging. I decided I should leave the U.S. government. Upon my return to the United States, I went to New York City for an interview with the Ford Foundation.

Richard Nixon was elected president in November 1968, two weeks before I went for the Ford Foundation interview. One day after that interview, Senator Edward Brooke called me. My brother Clarence, a senior advisor to the senator in Washington DC, had mentioned to the senator my intention to leave the U.S. government. The senator had another suggestion. He noted, "There is a possibility that you could work in the White House."

As a result of that conversation, I worked for six weeks at the president-elect's transition office in the Hotel Pierre in New York City. Then, with amazing speed, I moved to the White House, where I worked from January 20, 1968, until August 1971. For two and a half years, I worked in the West Wing for President Nixon's special assistant for appointments. Dwight Chapin (yes, one of those who did not escape the Watergate-related scandal and prison sentences) was my boss. My desk was directly outside the door to the Oval Office. To my right was the entrance to the Cabinet Room. I had a "front desk" at the White House, as the *Boston Globe* reported. That exposure significantly enhanced my self-confidence. Daily contact with cabinet members, heads of state, foreign ministers, leading businessmen, academics, and journalists taught me not to be intimidated by anyone.

When I moved to Washington I took up residence in the studio apartment that my brother Clarence had rented in Capitol Park–Southwest DC. Again my brothers saved the day, since I did not need to go apartment hunting when I returned to DC from New York. It was just what I wanted. My work at the White House meant I had little free time. I did not need any more space, and Clarence left it totally furnished. I still have Clarence's lounge chair in my Orlando residence. Furniture made in those days was sturdy.

One evening I went to pick up my mail at the Capitol Park complex, where I met Yvonne Franklin. We struck up a conversation because she looked so much like my dearest friend, Lorene Douglas McCain. Thus began another friendship of more than four decades. She recently retired as a senior flight attendant for United Airlines. She holds a special place in my heart. She knew me long before I ever held a diplomatic title. We were both rather naïve as to the harshness of the world, for we were grounded in Christian values that always look for the best in others. One of the first of our many trips together was to Nassau and a delightful visit with Mrs. Elma Jackson, a model and hairstylist and the one who taught etiquette to the "Teenettes." Oh, did we need that training. Mrs. Jackson, who had striking gray hair, was a tall and imposing figure. When she walked in a room, she owned it. She was another of the black female role models in my life.

As I watched television news coverage of the guests arriving at President Obama's first state dinner in honor of the president of India, I recalled my delight as I attended the "after dinner" performance for a state dinner in honor of France's president Georges Pompidou during the Nixon administration. White House staffers responsible for the event knew I had lived in Paris for three years prior to my work in the West Wing. They wisely thought I would be particularly honored to attend. I was. My date for the evening was Judge David Nelson of Boston. It was truly a thrill of a lifetime. The White House photographer, Ollie Atkins, gave me photos to mark that occasion.

Of course, not all major social events at the White House were for happy occasions. President Dwight D. Eisenhower passed away

March 28, 1969. Heads of state came from around the world to pay traditional condolence calls. Most of the guests entered the Oval Office from the Roosevelt Room. For some reason, President Charles de Gaulle did not. I remember this imposing French general standing in front of my desk as President Nixon came out to greet him. Their entire conversation was in English. I was absolutely flabbergasted. During my three years in Paris, I got the distinct impression that de Gaulle did not speak English.

In December 1969, only a month after the My Lai massacre of hundreds of Vietnamese civilians by U.S. troops, the nation held its first draft lottery since World War II and ended college draft deferments. Many had thought the unpopular war was winding down when in the spring of 1970 the president gave a television address announcing his expansion of the Vietnam War into Cambodia. Within days, students on college campuses across the nation took to the streets in protest. On May 4, after several days of unrest and violence in the college town of Kent, Ohio, troops of the Ohio National Guard fired sixty-seven rounds, killing four students and wounding nine others. The shots wounded some who were not part of the protests. Some protesters had been unruly, throwing rocks at the guardsmen, yelling insults, and ignoring orders to disperse. A presidential commission later concluded, "Indiscriminate firing of rifles into a crowd of students and the deaths that followed were unnecessary, unwarranted, and inexcusable." Just weeks after the deaths at Kent State, Neil Young's "Ohio," with its mournful repeated line "Four dead in Ohio," was played nationwide.

More than five million students organized a national campus strike that closed at least a hundred colleges and universities. Among my photos from my time in the White House is one of a historic meeting that President Nixon had with the presidents of historically black colleges and universities (HBCUs). A few days after the shootings at Kent State, I received a call from my niece, then a student at Lincoln University in Pennsylvania. She indicated that the HBCU presidents were concerned about Nixon's military campaign into Cambodia and our continued involvement in the Vietnam War. These presidents feared similar protests and loss of young lives if President Nixon did not meet with them. I contacted John Ehrlichman, then chairman of the White House Domestic Council, and suggested such a meeting. Ehrlichman followed through with a written recommendation to the president for that meeting. I am happy to report the meeting took place. That session was one example of the public's shift against the war that prompted Nixon to withdraw his military invasion of Cambodia and bring the fighting in Vietnam to an end.

I also had an unexpected discussion on desegregation with President Nixon as I delivered documents to the president prior to his meeting with Negro leaders to discuss the issue. The *New York Times* of March 21, 1971, under the headline "Nixon Meets with G.O.P. Negro Aides," reported my one-hour "chat" with the president about my experiences in the Boston school system and my attitudes on integration of all public schools and related racial issues.

I have no idea what impact our chat had on the president, but soon after that he announced his plan for a comprehensive review of all desegregation court rulings since the historic case of *Brown v. Board of Education* in 1954. His administration would carry out the law of the land, despite violation of Supreme Court rulings by seven southern states: Alabama, Arkansas, Georgia, Louisiana, Mississippi, North Carolina, and South Carolina. Southern leaders met with Nixon's cabinet officers in the Roosevelt Room, across the hall from the Oval Office, and with the president in his office. The president also traveled to New Orleans to carry his message to the South. George P. Shultz, Nixon's secretary of labor, who would serve as secretary of state from 1982 to 1989, wrote an op-ed piece about his involvement in Nixon's effort that ran in the *New York Times* on January 8, 2003. Shultz credits the president with defusing tensions and ending segregation peacefully. Times columnist Tom Wicker, in his book *One of Us: Richard Nixon and the American Dream*, writes, "The Nixon administration accomplished more in 1970 to desegregate Southern school systems than had been done in the 16 previous years, or probably since."

During these years, I made two or three flights on one of the White House's fleet of military planes. The food service provided by the navy chefs surpassed my limited experience flying business and first class on U.S. airlines. Of course, this was a working plane, so it was well equipped with the then-modern Selectric typewriters. When we headed to San Clemente, I had no idea we were flying into John Birch country. It was clear; I was a novelty for the townspeople each time I went out to dine with my fellow White House colleagues.

Working at the White House had its perks, but those perks came with some long days. In short, it was not the ideal work situation to encourage outside socializing. Each time President Nixon had a press briefing in the Oval Office, all of the West Wing staffers remained until the briefing or presidential message had ended and until journalists from the three major networks had retrieved and packed up all of their cumbersome equipment. It was not unusual for us to leave the West Wing at 11:00 p.m. or later. In fact, one evening a gentleman called after one of my many long days and said, "Harriet Elam, if you cannot have a friendly phone conversation because you are always so tired from work, you need to find a new job!" He was right. Actually, my feigned fatigue was really because I did not wish to speak with him, but already the diplomat, I used my work as an excuse to keep the conversation short.

I began to notice that my friends and extended family members enjoyed the special access I was able to provide for White House tours. Some "friends" liked such perks from me, and many were not genuine friends. I contemplated my future and decided that high-profile access to dignitaries and most senior government officials would not compensate for the constrained social life of a young woman in her late twenties. I decided it was time for me to move on.

In 1971 I resigned from my White House assignment to return to a more conventional U.S. government job in the State Department's Bureau of Education and Cultural Affairs. Before I left, my mother and my brothers Harry and Clarence were invited to the White House to meet President Nixon. The brief visit on February 19, 1971, included a photo opportunity. My brothers received coasters and cufflinks and my mother a stunning brooch. Each time I look at the photo of my dear mother beaming to have been in the

White House, I think of how thrilled she would be to know that Mrs. Marion Robinson, Michelle Obama's mother, resided with the First Family in the White House.

The lasting treasures of my White House assignment are the photos, a letter from President Nixon, and another handwritten congratulation letter from Dwight Chapin. In the typed letter signed by the president, Richard Nixon expressed his appreciation for the "splendid job" I had done but also for "the ready smile and bright eyes that invariably greeted me outside the Oval Office which helped to make each day a sunnier one whatever the weather."

The president, however, was not going to have many sunny days. The burglaries at the Democratic National Committee headquarters in the Watergate building on May 28 and June 17, 1972, led to the scandal that forced Richard Nixon's resignation two years later. My former boss, Dwight Chapin, deputy assistant to the president during Watergate, would be convicted of perjury and would serve nine months in a medium-security federal prison.

4

Young, Black, Female, and
. . . from the White House

Young, gifted and black
We must begin to tell our young
There's a world waiting for you
This is a quest that's just begun

—NINA SIMONE and WELDON IRVINE,
"To Be Young, Gifted and Black"

Maybe I needed a little more "finishing." My résumé now included my
work at the U.S. embassy in Paris and at the White House; however,
I was not exactly a worldly, cultured woman. I still had my moments
At the Bureau of Education and Cultural Affairs, my boss was Jim
Donovan, a fine man old enough to be my father. For some reason,
a bit of "the little Elam girl" came out one day when I said to him,
"Jim, you've been working longer than I am old." I was thirty-two
at the time and had no idea I would retire after forty-two years of
service. With a slight frown that turned into an accepting smile, he
responded, "Young lady, watch your language."

After a year in Jim Donovan's office, I worked in the Office of
Youth, Students, and Special Programs. This office was established to
help to expose many young American political leaders—Republicans,
Democrats, and Independents—to the sophisticated global political
scene. Spencer Oliver headed one of those groups, the American
Council of Young Political Leaders, and David Dorn headed another,
the United States Youth Council. The British Parliament and German

Bundestag had similar youth wings, and they also trained young leaders. We quickly learned that few of our "self-assured" young politicians could hold a candle to the erudite, well-read, and articulate young European leaders. Young Europeans were well versed in our political structure, and they were masters of the art of debate. I thought these interactions served as a great reality check for young American leaders. Together with Ambassador William Swing, I accompanied one of our delegations to Germany and the UK. Swing, in retirement, became the UN's director general for the International Organization on Migration. The trip took place in the early 1970s, when Europe and the United States faced student unrest and protests. I had seen student demonstrations on the Left Bank of Paris. Similar protests had spread to other European capitals. In the United States, the civil rights movement and hippy counterculture attitudes encouraged a lot of young people to reject what they called the Establishment. The Department of State encouraged Oliver and Dorn in their efforts to expose more young American leaders to the challenges foreign youth organizations faced. At the same time this international interaction gave Oliver and Dorn sobering lessons. They needed better preparation on the history of their European counterparts. As Jack Zetkulic said, they got hosed by the young, well-informed European politicians. America's young political leaders of any party had plenty to learn, and fortunately, learn they did.

William Hodding Carter III, who became the State Department's spokesman, was a member of a delegation of young political leaders going to Japan. At the last minute, one participant canceled. Hodding thought it would be wise for me to join the delegation. I was not allowed to join the group, for the "powers that be" thought it would look too much like a conflict of interest. Ever since, I have held a warm place in my heart for Hodding Carter.

As program officer in the Office of Students, Youth, and Special Projects, I traveled to New York to meet with the director of the American Field Service, a well-known student exchange program. The American Field Service received State Department funding to increase the diversity of participants and to broaden its host family base to countries in Latin America, Africa, and Asia. High school students spent an academic year abroad. Another important goal of State Department funding was to highlight the advantages of democracy over communism. We were still in the Cold War era. Back then it wasn't the threat of youngsters being influenced by militant terrorists but the threat of their becoming sympathizers with communist regimes. We also wanted the host governments to have an accurate view of democracy as young leaders engaged in dialogue in school and during the inevitable social gatherings while in another country. The United States Youth Council, an umbrella organization for twenty national youth groups, collaborated with our offices and cosponsored seminars on major international and domestic issues. Young people were becoming more globally aware.

The Turkish invasion of Cyprus took place in 1974. Our office arranged the safe return of all American exchange students to the United States. After that crisis, I made another trip to New York to brief outgoing U.S. exchange students and their group leaders. This seemed like the perfect job for me at the time. Daily engagement on international issues with my peers was no doubt the catalyst that led to my decision to seriously pursue a Foreign Service career. Dr. Richard Arndt, then the office director, strongly encouraged me to become a cultural affairs officer. I was intrigued and took the next steps to become a career Foreign Service officer. I was then a Foreign Service Reserve officer, a class that has since been abolished. Reservists were available for overseas assignment but spent most of their careers in Washington. I began to study for the Foreign Service oral exam. At that point, given all the reading I did, I felt I was in graduate school.

Foreign Service officers serve at some 265 U.S. diplomatic missions, some at embassies and consulates around the world and others in Washington and elsewhere for the Department of State. The Departments of Agriculture and Commerce and the U.S. Agency for International Development have their own overseas contingents. Traditionally, their people are assigned at U.S. embassies abroad as well. The entrance process for State Department officers is far more complex now. Other government agencies have a different entry process.

No matter the process, by this time I had heightened self-esteem and considered myself very much like the title of Nina Simone's song "Young, Gifted and Black." I was going to ace the orals, and thanks to the tutoring and guidance of several senior black officers, I did.

I was always inspired when I listened to Nina Simone's song. For Christmas 1970, my brother Harry and his dear wife, Barbara, gave me Lorraine Hansberry's work of the same title. Their inscription in that book reads, "You are young, gifted and black—and most importantly, you care. Your caring, your loving spirit, your warmth, your joy of life endear you to those whose lives you touch. Your bright shining personality and deep concern sustain, enrich and nurture all of us."

Although I recognize the family bias in the flattery, the message was particularly meaningful to me at the time. With a slight change in Nina Simone's lyrics, the song gained even greater significance. As I entered my new professional home at the venerable Department of State, I was not welcomed with open arms. I was young, black, female, . . . and a former secretary from the White House. My new State colleagues were not interested in my undergraduate Simmons degree in international relations. As a black officer and a female officer, I faced two glass ceilings in the Foreign Service. Many of the older civil servants were not at all thrilled with my arrival. From the outset, I noted how they were subtly unsupportive of any initiative I suggested, no matter how valid. Upon reflection, I honestly believe my challenges stemmed more from being a woman than from being black. To add insult to injury, I came from the White House, which was not, in their view, a badge of honor. Well aware of that bias, I immediately worked to establish credibility, especially since many were far more senior to me in age as well as being experienced civil servants.

My secretary was my mother's age and deserved my respect. My brothers reminded me that I could learn so much from experienced professionals. I treated each person with dignity and respect, turning the tense situation around. In time my colleagues came to respect and acknowledge my work. Dorothy Alexander, one of my former secretaries in the Office of Youth, Students, and Special Programs, now lives in Boca Raton. She turned 102 in 2017, and we remain in touch on birthdays and holidays. I continue to marvel at her clarity, her positive spirit, and her joie de vivre. Dottie continues to ballroom dance twice a week and drives, albeit cautiously.

I was the only African American in that State Department office. There were, however, African Americans in relatively senior positions at the State Department and U.S Agency for International Development (USAID) at that time. Richard Fox was the executive director of the Bureau of Educational and Cultural Affairs and later became ambassador to Trinidad and Tobago. William Jones, who would become ambassador to Haiti, was the deputy assistant secretary in Cultural Affairs. Our future ambassador to Liberia and South Africa, Edward J. Perkins, served in the Near East Asia executive director's office. Another career diplomat, William B. Davis, a Russian and Czech speaker, directed the Office of Exhibits for the USIA. Davis, who did not suffer fools, was my drill sergeant as I prepared for the Foreign Service oral exam. I also knew I had to be prepared before I entered a meeting with him regarding overseas exhibits for my posts.

Three of these gentlemen (Fox, Perkins, and Davis), along with Roburt Dumas, then director of USIA's Personnel Department, prepared me for the Foreign Service oral exam. At the time, I thought they were unmerciful as they drilled me for the exam. Not only did they provide me with a heavy reading list, they asked questions based on issues not included in their assigned readings. Yet the drilling paid off. I endured the three hours of the oral exam before a panel of diplomats and soon learned I passed. (It is seven hours today!) I shall be forever in debt to those demanding gentlemen.

A week prior to the oral exam, I was promoted to the next higher grade at USIA. However, the Board of Examiners did not accept that new grade after I passed the examination. I had to accept entrance at the lower grade. This was yet another indirect message to women and minority candidates.

Later I came to know these gentlemen (Fox, Perkins, Davis, and Dumas) even better through the Thursday Luncheon Group, a mentoring program founded in 1977 by senior black Foreign Service officers. Its founders, Davis and Dumas, chose what they considered an innocuous and nonthreatening name for the organization at that time. In 1977 State would have felt uneasy about any affinity group. Now there are LGBT groups, women's groups, Asian American groups, and Latino groups. In the midseventies, State viewed any group that might pressure or lobby for equal rights as threatening.

These men were the trailblazers for African Americans currently in the U.S. Foreign Service. I noted earlier that William "Bill" Davis not only spoke Russian but also was conversant in Czech. When Madeleine Albright, who is of Czech descent and speaks the language, became the first secretary of state to address the Thursday Luncheon Group in 1989, Davis and I were seated to her right. She was duly impressed when he spoke to her in Czech. As I observed that interaction, I became even more excited about my burgeoning Foreign Service career.

John Anderegg, who is not African American, showed his long-term commitment to the Thursday Luncheon Group. Over the years I observed his genuine support for merited career advancement of the group's members. John succeeded Jim Donovan as my boss at the Bureau of Education and Cultural Affairs. (Jim is the chap I described as having worked longer than I was old.) Anderegg was a trailblazer in his own way by becoming openly affiliated with an African American organization in the mid-1970s.

There were very few senior women in the Foreign Service at that time, but I had Mary Pearl Dougherty, my surrogate mother and mentor since my years in Paris.

My first overseas assignment as a career Foreign Service officer took me to Dakar, Senegal, as assistant cultural affairs officer. This, however, was not my first trip to Africa. In 1968 my brother Clarence took me to Senegal. Clarence had accompanied Senator Brooke as part of a congressional delegation a year earlier. Gorée Island, off the coast of Dakar, has major historical significance for African Americans. From this island, and to a greater extent the ports at what today are Ghana and Benin, Africans were forced onto slave ships bound to British, French, Spanish, Dutch, and Portuguese colonies in the Americas in the seventeenth and eighteenth centuries. Historians differ on just how many of the twelve million Africans forced into slavery departed from Gorée Island, citing other major slave ports, but in 1962 Maison des Esclaves (House of Slaves) opened in a reconstructed memorial "Door of No Return" for Africans doomed to the Atlantic slave trade. By accompanying Senator Brooke's congressional delegation, my brother and I, just a few generations separated from the Lees and Elams who had taken slave names from their South Carolina and Virginia plantation owners, were retracing the steps of our forebears.

When I returned to Dakar in 1975 as assistant cultural attaché at the embassy, I was determined that I would not have any "servant" working for me. After all, I came with the heavy cultural baggage of having grown up in segregated America. Although my father had been an auto mechanic, my dear mother was, in essence, a servant as she cleaned homes to supplement my father's income. I had no idea I was going to learn another life lesson from my early insistence on doing everything myself as a young diplomat.

Kebe was the Gambian cook who had worked at the cultural attaché's residence for many years. When I arrived, I said I did not need a cook. I did not want anyone working for me at the residence. Psychologically, I just could not bear the thought. After two months, the senior Foreign Service national (an earlier term for indigenous employees who worked at American embassies; now they are identified as locally employed staff) approached me. "Miss Elam," he said, "you are really ruining the economy of Senegal." Kebe, after longtime embassy employment, was unable to support his family. That observation resonated with me. I could not run exchange programs and entertain Senegalese nationals and visiting U.S. dignitaries without some help. I relented and hired Kebe. What a positive addition he was to my lifestyle in Dakar. He spoke about five languages. Originally from The Gambia, where the British had trained him, Kebe was an elegant gent who carried himself with a quiet dignity I admired. He might have been a cook, but his comportment defied all stereotypical images I previously held. His pride and poise, like those of so many Africans I met, were constant reminders, as an African American, that I had much to learn from Africans who had long histories and cultures that instilled that sense of pride.

I welcomed Kebe's expertise, but I still could not bear to ring a bell to have him come and clear the table after courses. We worked out our own code for when it was time to clear the table. In my subsequent posts, the dining room had a rug where we installed a small buzzer system to alert the cook when it was time to clear the table. To this day I won't ring a bell because too many of my ancestors were on the other end of such bells.

My job description included tutoring Senegalese president Léopold Sédar Senghor in English. A poet and political leader before Senegal won its independence from France, Senghor was a cultural icon in Europe and Africa and served as president for two decades. I was absolutely mortified by the challenge. He had been the first and only African elected to the Académie Française, a French literary organization. At that point in my career, I had not taught anyone anything. I certainly had not taught a head of state. Ambassador Frances Dee Cook, who became our ambassador to Burundi, Cameroun, and Oman, had just left Dakar as cultural attaché. She had been President Senghor's English tutor. Fortunately, the late Blake Robinson, a former Fulbright director in Liberia and an African studies scholar, was named cultural attaché for Dakar. To my relief, Blake taught President Senghor English.

The work environment in the Cultural Section of our embassy in Dakar was difficult, thanks to a boss insecure around younger Foreign Service officers (FSOs) who had a broad knowledge of American culture and literature. He had been a journalist, as were many USIA officers early on. He possessed limited interpersonal skills. Determined to prove my capabilities, despite the hostile environment, I completed my tour. My frequent contact with Senegalese academics, journalists, and other professionals during our cultural programs made the office work environment bearable. Also, the U.S. ambassador at that time was O. Rudolph Aggrey, an African American of Ghanaian descent. Aggrey was a scholar and diplomat for whom I had the highest respect. For years I had read about Aggrey and was pleased I had been assigned to an embassy under his direction. My official Foreign Service commission arrived while I was in Senegal, and Ambassador Aggrey presided at my swearing-in ceremony. To return to that post twenty-eight years later as ambassador and sit in the very office where Ambassador Aggrey sat was absolutely amazing.

During my first tour in Dakar, I was frustrated with my attempts to set up an American studies program. Each time I approached an official at the Ministry of Education, I was required to first meet with the French *conseiller tecnique* (technical advisor). In 1975 Senegal still was a very young independent nation. It seemed to me that the French remained somewhat in control of all ministries for many years. Each ministry had a technical advisor, and that office was right next to the minister's. I was convinced that these advisors used all means possible to thwart our attempts to secure Senegalese approval for American studies programs.

In order to circumvent the influence of the French technical advisors, I used representational events to converse directly with ministers. During these social gatherings, I explained the value of American studies (literature, science, the arts, and culture) and highlighted the benefit of American professors sharing their knowledge of Senegalese literature, the arts, and culture with Senegalese students in an environment where both could learn from each other.

I also told my Senegalese interlocutors that the programming I would arrange would include respected speakers on the U.S. civil rights movement. The road to establishing an American studies program at the University of Dakar was painfully slow, but eventually we succeeded. Imagine my delight upon my return to Dakar as ambassador when I gave the closing speech at the Nineteenth Anniversary American Studies Conference at the University of Dakar. Approximately 250 participants from other universities in sub-Saharan Africa attended. My work at representational events in Dakar twenty-eight years earlier had borne fruit.

Senegalese scholars and American studies specialists remained on my mind when I attended the Salzburg American Studies Seminar in Austria in 2010. I was concerned when I saw no participants from sub-Saharan Africa. Upon my return to the United States, I made a commitment to ensure there would be a Senegalese participant at future sessions of that prestigious seminar. As with everything reliant on U.S. government regulations, it took a couple of years for my wonderful colleagues in the Cultural Affairs Section of the American embassy in Dakar to successfully send a participant to the seminar. Reports of Senegalese representation in 2013 were so positive that I was inspired to continue support for a 2015 participant.

While in Senegal during my first tour, I was sent to Mali on temporary duty (three months) as acting public affairs officer while the post awaited the designation of a replacement. It was an opportunity to serve in this history-rich African nation. I traveled to Timbuktu and Mopti, where I viewed the remains of universities that existed well before the oldest U.S. universities. Sadly, many of Mali's historic sites were destroyed in the 2012 civil war.

In Mali I worked closely with the ministers of culture and education on educational exchange programs. I found it a curious and disquieting coincidence that the senior foreign national assistant in the Public Affairs Office was the niece of the Malian president. American FSOs had to be circumspect in any reference to the current Malian government. It was not the ideal work situation. The president's niece was a tall, imposing woman and walked with grace, pride, and dignity. I dared not destroy the credibility of our program by an inappropriate reference to the Malian government or culture. I might have been too careful and too diplomatic. The Malians responded positively to the programs that I coordinated during my short stay. Fortunately, we did not have any major political crises at that time. There was often skepticism about the United States in the developing world. The sheer existence of a public diplomacy program that resulted in heightened interest in the United States was considered an accomplishment.

I remember wondering why in the world the public affairs officer's residence would have a swimming pool, since the water supply was minimal and the pool remained dry throughout my temporary assignment. Electricity was sporadic, which meant air conditioning and lights were equally unreliable. Even when we had power, Malian television could not begin to match the three major networks most enjoyed in the United States. With plenty of time to read, I had to overcome the challenge of sporadic electricity. I relied on my flashlight. I did not have a kerosene lamp, which my husband used as he grew up on the island of Grenada, but I am sure it would have been a welcomed addition in Bamako. A USAID colleague advised that I carry flashlights wherever I traveled on the continent and that I carry a higher wattage lightbulb with me to use in hotel rooms. The voice of experience was a welcomed gift. At times I wondered if I had returned to the Dark Ages.

When I returned to Senegal, I must admit, I thought I had returned to civilization. Yet my visits to Foreign Service national employees' homes near Bamako allowed me to personally experience Mali's local traditions and cuisine. I must admit it took a while for me to get used to eating everything laced with sand. And on my first visit to the meat market in Bamako, I was horrified when I saw flies covering huge slabs of meat. I became a vegetarian overnight.

Although I did not recall having made a noteworthy impact during my three-month stint in Bamako, Chargé Stephen Dawkins indicated that the relationships established through my strategically targeted programs in Mali proved beneficial to the embassy's work for the remainder of that year. In 1994 Dawkins spoke to the members of my senior seminar class. Again, he commented positively on my 1976 temporary assignment to Bamako. I felt somewhat as I felt when I graduated from high school. It seemed I did something right.

In the late summer of 1976, I returned to DC. The European area director, Jodie Lewinson, asked that I consider an assignment as branch public affairs officer in Milan, Italy. Few African American Foreign Service officers were offered European assignments. In those days, it was unusual for African American officers to have assignments outside of Africa, the Caribbean, or some parts of Latin America. I cannot believe that I actually turned down that assignment. I told Lewinson I was happy in French-speaking Africa. At that point, I had no desire to learn Italian. I had no idea that I would eventually learn Greek and Turkish.

My second full-time assignment, after the three-month tour in Mali, was in Abidjan, Côte d'Ivoire, or as it was also called, the Ivory Coast. I served under the brilliant tutelage of Ambassador Monteagle "Monty" Stearns. This U.S. ambassador and his wife were genuinely involved with all sectors of the Ivoirian community. The Ivoirians respected, admired, and loved them. Remember, this was in the mid-1970s, a time when the United States was experiencing significant racial tensions. Here I was, working abroad with a white ambassador who was a wonderful combination of East Coast reserve and West Coast openness. Although he was a Harvard graduate who had significant exposure to those who attended elite institutions, Stearns was raised in Carmel, California. His wife, Toni, attributed his easy rapport to his far more open-minded upbringing in Carmel. He treated all of the Africans with the utmost respect. As an African American imbued with America's ever-present obsession with race, I found it phenomenal to watch the Stearnses' interactions.

Fortunately, I was in the right place at the right time when the assignment officers needed a Foreign Service officer fluent in French for the Abidjan assignment. I had signed up for worldwide assignments, but I chose to return to Africa. I was aware of other horizons, but at that time, I was not savvy on how to bid strategically on assignments. Despite my naïveté, I thoroughly enjoyed my African postings. In those days, USIA Foreign Service officers were not required to bid on all geographic regions. Also, since the USIA officer corps was much smaller than the State Department's, the bidding process was less complicated.

For me, language was probably the dictating factor. I spoke French, so Abidjan was a natural follow-on post. As a capital city, Abidjan was considered a prime African assignment. The United States had considerable political and economic interest in the Ivory Coast because of its diverse economy. Abidjan was home to a major commodities trading board. The Ivoirians were savvy businessmen. From my observations, they were more French than the French. I found it curious that in hundred-degree temperatures, they were often attired in three-piece suits and did not sport traditional dress as often as the Senegalese. Their temperaments were far more complex, and I found their personalities more difficult to read and to understand than those of the Senegaleses.

As I continued to marvel at how Ambassador Stearns operated in Abidjan, I came to understand the important role diplomacy plays in foreign affairs when practiced by an expert. Stearns's speeches, his representational functions, and his daily schedule combined what I instinctively believed were the best diplomatic practices. My career goals became clear. I wanted to be like Ambassador Stearns. Stearns and his wife bridged cultural gaps. His fluent French, his knowledge of U.S. and Ivoirian history, and his engaging personality made him, in my mind, the consummate diplomat. When I speak with young Foreign Service officers, I encourage them to carefully observe senior officers they admire and learn from them. On the day the Stearnses departed, ministers, elected officials, and Ivorian business contacts came to the airport to bid them farewell. I had never before seen such an outpouring of respect. Stearns was always dignified. A former Marine, he stood ramrod straight. Later I was blessed to serve with Ambassador Stearns in Athens, Greece.

We remained close. My last visit to their Cambridge home was in April 2014, when they shared with me the prestigious award he received from the Greek government in March 2014, the Order of the Phoenix. Ambassador Stearns had lost his eyesight to macular degeneration and coped with inevitable health challenges. Yet he completed his third book in the spring of 2014 and celebrated his ninetieth birthday in December 2014. He died in May 2016. Their daughter, Emily, now serves in the State Department with her husband, Elliot Fertik, after their tandem diplomatic tour in Chennai, India. Emily says she credits my counsel with her success in passing the Foreign Service exam. When I think of what her father did for me, I was honored to share what expertise I had gained with such a capable and deserving candidate for the Foreign Service.

In the "glory days," Foreign Service posts had much larger staffs than today. In Abidjan, I had two cultural assistants. Coincidentally, both were African American males. They were intelligent, well read, and engaging. At times they thought they could charm their supervisor so that they would not be required to do the less glamorous tasks of our work, which might involve their evenings or weekends. William V. Parker and Don Q. Washington retired after notable diplomatic careers in Europe, Latin America, and Asia. As I followed their successes, I was very proud. My first dealings with them let me know I had to be a strict supervisor. I drafted candid evaluation reports on their work their first year in Abidjan. Both questioned me about my observations. In their early twenties, both perceived my candor as being too harsh on young African Americans in the Foreign Service. When they questioned my reports, I said, "If I am not honest with you, no one else will be." I continued, "This highly competitive system is set up for failure for the slightest deviation from the norm or for making unwise choices."

Besides keeping those gentlemen on track while in Abidjan, one of the most significant contributions I made to the post was to send a decidedly anti-American Ivoirian journalist to the States. His coverage of the United States exhibited unmasked skepticism about our foreign policy. Despite his blunt arrogance, I was determined to learn why he had such a negative view of the United States. Granted, justified skepticism of some of our foreign policy decisions exists worldwide. This chap had never visited the United States, so I asked him how he could make such critical assumptions without seeing the country with his own eyes. He could not offer a convincing response. The late John Garner, the public affairs officer in Abidjan, supported my nomination of the journalist for an International Visitor Grant. Garner was another Foreign Service officer who helped me learn how to manage a sizeable post. When he went on leave, he designated me as acting public affairs officer. I was very proud to take on that task and appreciated a boss who had such faith in me. John Garner taught me not to micromanage. He passed away several years ago, but his impact on my career prepared me to manage the 1999 USIA merger with State.

With John Garner's help, we moved the journalist's nomination through the committee. The journalist returned without becoming pro-American, but his reporting was less strident and more balanced.

The ambassador and our mission colleagues agreed there was value in his selection. The U.S. government gained more from this International Visitor Grant than if we had sent a pro-American Ivoirian.

The Ivory Coast's diverse ethnicity and its north-south divide have led to contentious standoffs between political rivals, stretching from the 1970s to more recent times, including former Ivoirian president Laurent Gbagbo's long-standing challenges to newly elected president Alassane Ouatarra. When I was posted there in the mid- to late 1970s the Ivoirians seemed to display less national pride than I had observed in Senegal. Since my assignment, I have learned that many Ivoirian citizens were not born there. They immigrated from nearby African nations and were warmly welcomed into the workforce. With close to a dozen indigenous languages and an equally large number of ethnic groups, French is their lingua franca. I was invited to the homes of senior contacts and attended plays in the languages of my host countries. My very presence improved America's image and our accessibility to pivotal members of the artistic and journalist communities.

Fortunately, French is the language used in all educational facilities, including the University of Abidjan. The university was very well appointed. In fact, it was more impressive than the University of Dakar. The French invested heavily in educational and other public institutions because Ivoirians had a viable and more diverse economy than other West African nations. Ivoirians wanted their students to be prepared to fill the many positions that would be open to them in the future. President Félix Houphouët-Boigny was a politician who had trained as a doctor and treated the rural poor. Although he was not a poet or an intellectual like Senegal's Senghor, the French considered him among the more respected elder statesmen of their former colonies.

After my time in the Ivory Coast, I applied for a fellowship from the U.S. Information Agency to attend the Fletcher School of Law and Diplomacy at Tufts University. Ambassador Stearns wrote what I thought was an incredible recommendation letter. I am sure that letter led to my selection as USIA's 1979 Jefferson Fellowship recipient.

I entered the Fletcher School in the fall of 1979, but the summer before I entered graduate school, I went to Bermuda to visit Dick Saunders and his wife, Emily. Dick was the chief photographer and an editor of USIA's *TOPIC* magazine. I traveled with Cheryl Dobbins, who had been one of the first female speakers I programmed when I was cultural attaché in Abidjan in 1977–79. Our friendship survived her embarrassing attempt to get through airport security without her forgotten passport by taking on Butterfly McQueen's southern accent as Prissy, Scarlett O'Hara's maid in the 1939 film *Gone with the Wind*. Attempting to bluff her way through customs as *my maid*, she went into her silly act: "Missy, I'm so sorry. I forgot my passport!" I thought she'd lost her mind. She stayed in that character for the next ten minutes, using that high-pitched voice and telling the airport officials, "She know I'm all right" and implying she worked for me. I was ready to kill her. Eventually, her driver's license was good enough to get into Bermuda. Butterfly McQueen's "I don't know nothin' 'bout birthin' babies!" might have sealed her fame as an actor, but she did not relish the demeaning role. Although Cheryl and I joke about it now, when it happened, I was not thrilled to have been put in that position.

In 1980 I earned a master's degree in public diplomacy. The program was rigorous. When I think about it, I don't quite know how I managed. I became a hermit, studied four hours each night after classes, and had limited phone contact with family and friends. I was in Boston, near many dear family members, but I could spend minimal time with them, for my first priority was graduate study. I had to get the master's degree.

Dr. Willard Johnson, a tenured professor of political science at Massachusetts Institute of Technology, taught U.S. Policy toward Southern Africa. Johnson was the first and only African American professor I ever had. He was invited to teach because students of every color said they did not see any diversity among the faculty at Tuft's Fletcher School.

Dr. Johnson's overall focus was on the African continent, and his classes were always overenrolled. Finally, I had another new role model in academia. Here was someone who looked like me and was

Fig. 1. Robert and Blanche Elam pose with their three
sons outside their Boston home. Author's collection.

Fig. 2. (*above*) Harriet Elam's senior photo for the class of 1959 at Roxbury Memorial High School for Girls. Author's collection.

Fig. 3. (*opposite top*) Harriet Elam and her mother in front of their home at 340 Walnut Avenue, Roxbury, following Harriet's June 1959 graduation. Author's collection.

Fig. 4. (*opposite bottom*) An undated photo of the Elams around the family table. Author's collection.

Fig. 5. (*opposite top*) The five Elam siblings gather at Elam-Thomas's condo at the Park Sutton in Silver Spring, Maryland, in February 1983, just prior to her assignment to Athens. Author's collection.

Fig. 6. (*opposite bottom*) Elam-Thomas's parents before their fiftieth anniversary celebration. Author's collection.

Fig. 7. (*above*) Elam-Thomas at her desk, with the door to the Oval Office in the background on the right. U.S. National Archives, Collection RN-WHPO.

Fig. 8. (*above*) Richard Nixon is all smiles as Elam-Thomas shares a private moment with the president on February 20, 1971. U.S. National Archives, Collection RN-WHPO.

Fig. 9. (*opposite top*) Elam-Thomas with Allan Goodman, the author of *The Goodman Report*, which in the 1980s brought attention to the need to recruit women and minorities into the senior ranks of the American Foreign Service, September 18, 2011. Author's collection.

Fig. 10. (*opposite bottom*) Elam-Thomas briefing participants in a group exchange program at Abidjan, Côte d'Ivoire, in the mid-1970s. Author's collection.

Fig. 11. (*above*) The wedding party at Peoples Congregational Church, Washington DC, on October 3, 1999, with Mary Dougherty to the left of the bride and groom and Barbara and Harry Elam on the right. Author's collection.

Fig. 12. (*opposite top*) Elam-Thomas at her desk at the U.S. embassy, Dakar, Senegal. Author's collection.

Fig. 13. (*opposite bottom*) Chief of Protocol Bruno Diatta and Elam-Thomas review the honor guard as she arrives at the Palais Présidentiel in Dakar, Senegal, to present her credentials as the new U.S. ambassador on January 14, 2000. Author's collection.

Fig. 14. (*opposite top*) Elam-Thomas beams after presenting her credentials, as Senegalese president Abdou Diouf (*left*) shakes hands with Wilfred Thomas. Author's collection.

Fig. 15. (*opposite bottom*) Elam-Thomas in traditional Senegalese dress during a November 7, 2002, visit to a classroom at Rufisque, a western Senegal suburb of Dakar. Her purple dress was a gift from the village. Author's collection.

Fig. 16. (*above*) President Bill Clinton with Elam-Thomas at the Little Rock Nine fiftieth anniversary at Central High School, Little Rock, Arkansas, September 2007. Author's collection.

Fig. 17. (*top*) Elam-Thomas in 1988 with her first braids, which changed "my look for the rest of my life. I sat in Elin LaVar's chair for eight hours as she braided my hair. I came out a new person. The braids had a subtle dignity about them. All of a sudden, I felt comfortable in my own skin. I wasn't the diplomat who is black trying to be white." Author's collection.

Fig. 18. (*bottom*) Elam-Thomas conducts a business etiquette session with UCF Global Perspectives interns and fellows. Author's collection.

Fig. 19. Justin Davis, the chief of the political section in Havana, with Elam-Thomas on July 1, 2015, the day President Barack Obama told the nation of his plans to reopen the U.S. embassy in Havana and restore diplomatic relations with Cuba. Elam-Thomas, who had encouraged Davis to pursue a career in international affairs, experienced the instant gratification of knowing the next generation shared her commitment to diplomacy. Author's collection.

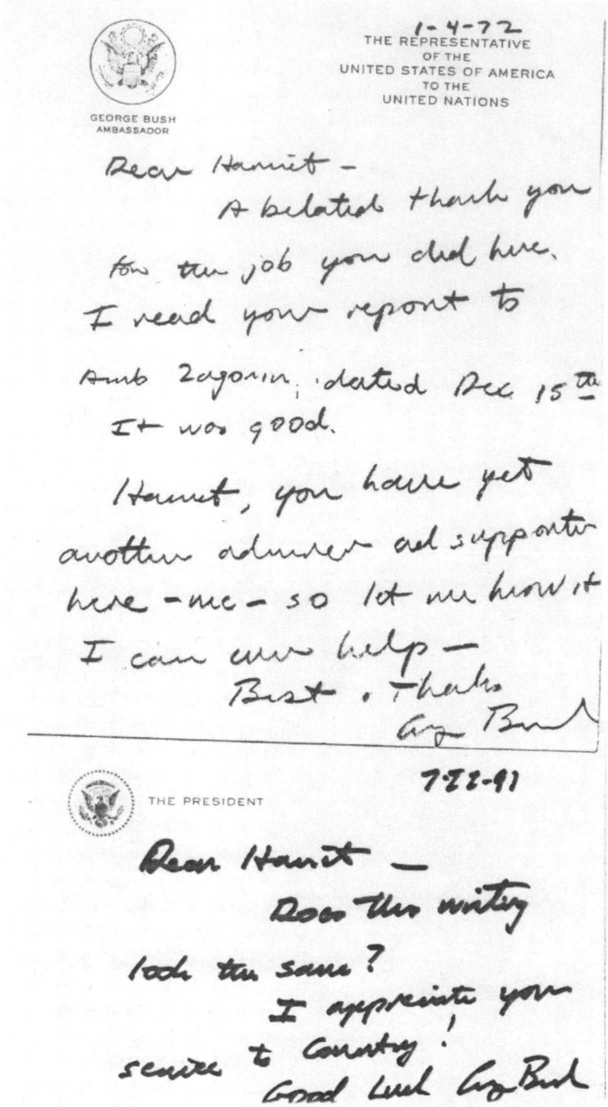

Fig. 20. Two notes to Elam-Thomas from George H. W. Bush, the top one written when he was the U.S. ambassador to the United Nations and the other when he was president, in which he jokes about his handwriting. Author's collection.

March 5, 1971

Dear Mr. President:

Although I had been involved in the preparation
of your daily schedule for the past two years,
I had a very special feeling when I had the
opportunity to introduce you to members of my
family two weeks ago.

You can imagine what a heart-warming and
thrilling and thrilling experience it was for
someone of my mother's generation to meet the
President of The United States. I am most
appreciative for your taking time to see some
of the Elam Family prior to my departure from
The White House.

The pearl pin which you gave me is of special
significance and value to me for I know who some
of the recipients have been in the past. Your
letter, which I received upon my return from
Boston, is one which I shall cherish always.

Thank you, Mr. President, for all of the
kindnesses which you extended to me during the
time I spent as a member of your staff. And, a
special thank you for allowing me to have this
fascinating and unique experience.

Sincerely,

Harriet Elam

Fig. 21. Elam-Thomas wrote this personal note to President Nixon,
thanking him for the kindness shown to her family members when
they visited the White House. Author's collection.

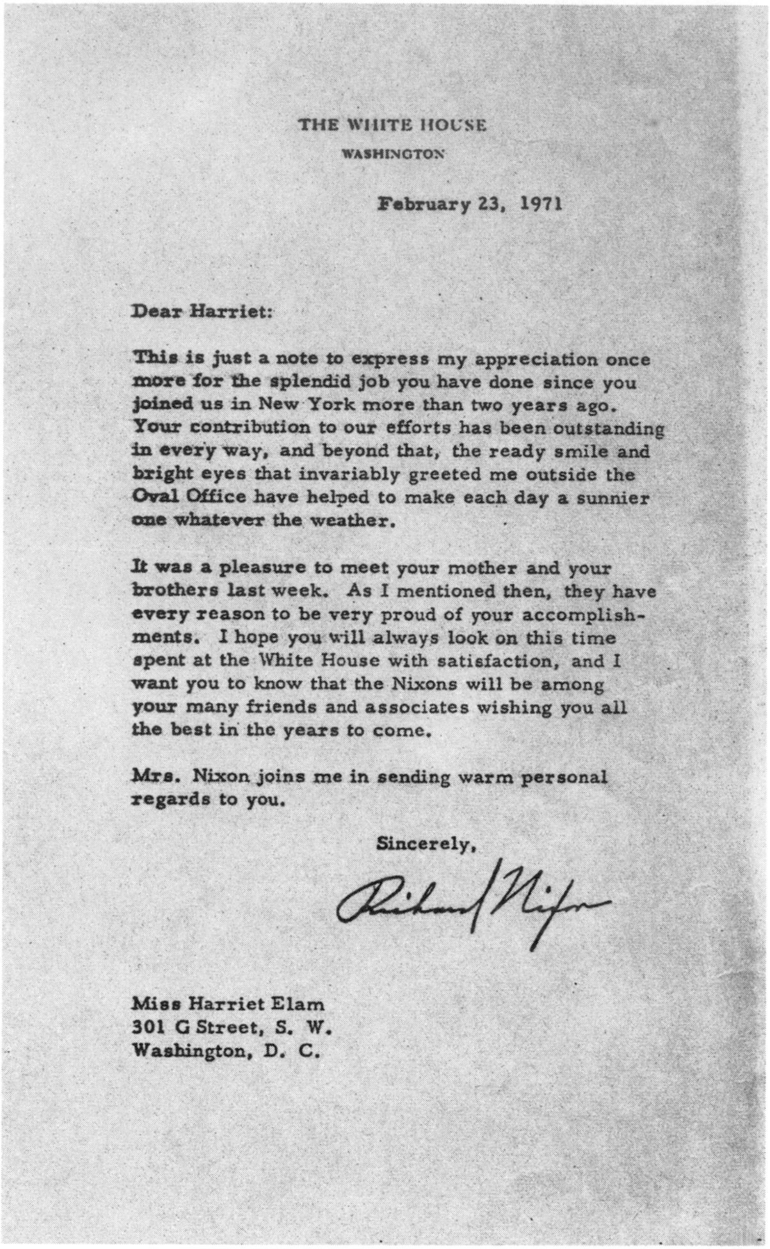

THE WHITE HOUSE
WASHINGTON

February 23, 1971

Dear Harriet:

This is just a note to express my appreciation once
more for the splendid job you have done since you
joined us in New York more than two years ago.
Your contribution to our efforts has been outstanding
in every way, and beyond that, the ready smile and
bright eyes that invariably greeted me outside the
Oval Office have helped to make each day a sunnier
one whatever the weather.

It was a pleasure to meet your mother and your
brothers last week. As I mentioned then, they have
every reason to be very proud of your accomplishments. I hope you will always look on this time
spent at the White House with satisfaction, and I
want you to know that the Nixons will be among
your many friends and associates wishing you all
the best in the years to come.

Mrs. Nixon joins me in sending warm personal
regards to you.

Sincerely,

Richard Nixon

Miss Harriet Elam
301 G Street, S. W.
Washington, D. C.

Fig. 22. Richard M. Nixon's kind words to Elam-Thomas
when she left the White House. Author's collection.

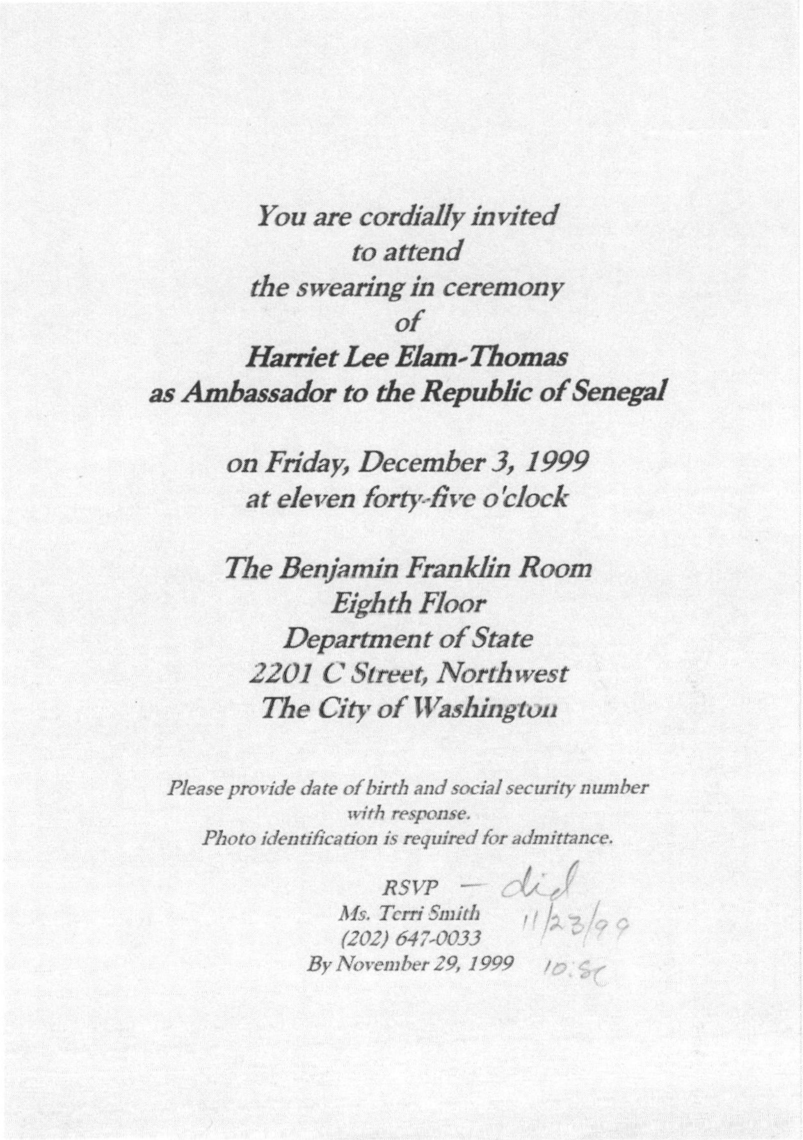

You are cordially invited
to attend
the swearing in ceremony
of
Harriet Lee Elam-Thomas
as Ambassador to the Republic of Senegal

on Friday, December 3, 1999
at eleven forty-five o'clock

The Benjamin Franklin Room
Eighth Floor
Department of State
2201 C Street, Northwest
The City of Washington

Please provide date of birth and social security number
with response.
Photo identification is required for admittance.

RSVP — did
Ms. Terri Smith   11/23/99
(202) 647-0033
By November 29, 1999   10.5c

Fig. 23. An invitation to Elam-Thomas's swearing-in ceremony
as ambassador to Senegal. Author's collection.

Prof. Iba Der Thiam
University Professor
Former Minister
Deputy at National Assembly
Secretary General of Political Party
CDP-Garab Gi

Your Excellency:

As you are getting ready to return home after your tour of duty in Senegal, I would like to express to you my satisfaction for the way you have strengthened the long lasting and fruitful relationship between your country and Senegal, through your humanism, human relations and your contacts with different strata of the Senegalese society.

Many Senegalese will miss you, as you were all smiles, gracious, tolerant and brotherly. Thanks to you, the image of the American people compels recognition to all as a courageous people, hard working, obstinate, an advocate of freedoms and also a nation which protects the weak.

Your contribution has been all the more appreciated as the United States has, for a long time, embodied for African States the model of an important allied in their fight for independency. President Trumann is the one who declared earlier that "time for colonial empires was over". He was the first to have put forward the idea to "help poor countries".

I am deeply convinced that the United States of America has a mission, that of a precursor people, bearer of a very high humanism for peace; a mission to guide the world with justice, to lead the way, to show the path to happiness, prosperity, security, mutual understanding, and peace.

I wish you a safe return to your country.

Professor Iba Der Thiam

Fig. 24. A farewell letter from Professor Iba Der Thiam, first vice president of the National Assembly during Elam-Thomas's time in Senegal. Author's collection.

absolutely brilliant. All of the students wanted to please him, and we worked doubly hard to get good grades. Our classmates included Liberia's former minister of finance, the son of Ethiopia's minister of education, and an eventual Greek minister.

During one of the first sessions in the international economics course, I thought it odd that a good number of the American students, many of them Ivy Leaguers, did not know what an exchange rate was. Many of these were from some of the top schools in the United States. I breathed a sigh of relief and said to myself, I think I will get through this course.

At Fletcher, most students were in their early twenties and straight out of undergraduate school. I was thirty-eight years old. It was a challenge made harder because while at Fletcher, my almost six-year relationship with a USAID colleague ended. My classmates helped me weather that storm and supported me during my final exams. They organized study groups and frequently reminded me that I *was* going to finish Fletcher. It was a grueling time. I would not care to repeat that experience.

I was inspired to do my best because I did not want to disappoint Dr. Johnson. He was probably prouder of me than I was of myself when he attended the Simmons College commencement fifteen years later to watch me receive an honorary doctorate. Ambassador Stearns and his wife were there as well.

Dr. Johnson would become cofounder of TransAfrica, which in the 1990s was the largest American antiapartheid group calling for Nelson Mandela's release from prison in South Africa. Dr. Johnson, now an MIT professor emeritus, and his wife, Dr. Vivian Johnson, maintain a primary residence in Newton, Massachusetts, and a winter home in Sarasota, Florida. While at their Sarasota home, his presentations to Ringling College classes informed the students of the antiapartheid movement and of the efforts to free Nelson Mandela. Johnson spent more than three decades in classrooms, but he also took to the streets. He once was arrested for leading Boston protests against South Africa's racial separation policies. My Fletcher professor remains one of the leaders of the Boston Pan-African Forum, which promotes relations between the United States and the countries and peoples of Africa and the African diaspora.

Just recently, on the anniversary of Mandela's 1990 release after twenty-seven years in prison, my thoughts turned to Professor Johnson. Perhaps because he was my brother's friend for many years, I had worked doubly hard not to disappoint him. He did for me what I would do for the young African American Foreign Service officers I would subsequently supervise. He held me to a higher standard, knowing the competition was tough. He wanted me to be prepared.

After I completed all of the academic requirements for my master's degree, I took the French language test. One of my classmates was a United Nations interpreter, and we conversed frequently in French. Fletcher did not have language instructors separate from the Tufts Language Department. Instead, a French-speaking economics professor administered the exam. I did not complete the written portion of the exam to his satisfaction.

I had served for seven years in French-speaking countries. The Foreign Service Institute had rated me as superior in general language-learning proficiency. And I had received the coveted 3/3 (the working-level speaking and reading rating) in French from the Foreign Service Institute (FSI) on that language exam before I went to Senegal.

After my second attempt, I passed the written and oral portions of the French exam administered by the same professor. Coincidentally, that professor, Dr. Abdul Aziz, would eventually come to Athens on a speaker program because he was a friend of the public affairs officer in Athens.

I continued to wonder, if I met the State Department's French-language requirements to serve overseas, how could this professor prevent me from obtaining that master's degree? The experience showed me that academia can be very political. Something was going on; however, I could not put my finger on it. I decided not to return to Fletcher for a doctorate. When I graduated in 1980, I knew that if I ever got a doctorate, it would have to be an honorary one. I had no idea that years later I would receive four honorary doctorates.

I returned to Washington as a career counselor in USIA Personnel after graduating from the Fletcher School. I wondered why I was assigned to be a career counselor. After all, I had just studied foreign policy, conflict resolution, and international relations. I soon realized that conflict resolution and finding the right person for the assignment required career counselor expertise.

I remember a midlevel officer who was one of my clients and was on the threshold of entering the Senior Foreign Service. When his name was not on the promotion list, he came to my office, terribly depressed. He felt his career was no longer worth pursuing. He had faced many personal and professional challenges. In essence, he announced that his life was not worth living because he did not make it into the Senior Foreign Service. He dashed out of my office filled with anxiety. I followed him down the stairs and stopped him. I said, "No profession should define you. Nothing you have experienced thus far in life merits the action you are considering." None of us can second-guess the final choices of selection panels. I told him about other sobering challenges faced by USIA colleagues, one whose nine-year old child had just died of cancer and the government would not cover the cost of flying the family back to the United States to be together because the father was a month shy of the requirement for the government to cover the cost of a stateside trip. I fought for this family in personnel meetings but did not succeed in getting a waiver. These examples seemed to help him, and he calmly left the premises. This colleague remained in the service. Honestly, I was not trained for such experiences, but I draw on whatever is necessary during crises.

Many of my colleagues believed the system was not fair to single women. They saw evidence that posts at large embassies like Mexico City and Hong Kong were given to tandem couples. In those settings USIA did not have policies against one spouse supervising the other. One single female client said, "I am ready to learn Mandarin, but you're not going to send me to Beijing since it is a tandem post." She was correct. I did not have a satisfying response for her and accepted that I could not win all the battles. This one I knew I had not won.

Elinor Constable won. When she was planning her wedding, her superior expected her to follow tradition and resign from the Foreign Service. She had the nerve to tell the legendary Frances E. Willis, "If you want me out of the Foreign Service, you have to fire me." (Frances Willis would never marry, but she became the first woman to rise through the ranks of the Foreign Service to become an ambassador and the first woman to hold the title of career ambassador.)

During her own nearly forty-year career, Elinor Constable served as ambassador to Kenya in the late 1980s. She was the first woman principal deputy assistant secretary of the Economic Bureau and assistant secretary in the Bureau of Oceans, International Environmental and Scientific Affairs. But first, she had to challenge the Foreign Service traditions of the 1950s by refusing to resign when she married. She demanded to see the regulation requiring her to resign. There was no such regulation, just custom. Also, the government did not allow maternity leave at the time. Women were forced to make a choice: family or work. It seems there was a little Rosa Parks in Elinor Constable. She was tired of all the rules that made no sense to her. She stood her ground, and the Department of State backed off.

Allan E. Goodman has made it his life's work to see to it that the Foreign Service looks like America. He is the author of *The Goodman Report*, which brought attention to the need to recruit women and minorities by pointing out in the 1980s the underrepresentation of women and minorities in the senior ranks of the American Foreign Service. He pointed out that women and minorities were not allowed to move up in the Foreign Service in the mid-1980s. He spoke to the Thursday Luncheon Group and another created by women Foreign Service officers. That's when I first met him. I thought to myself, this white man has done all this research and he gets up and tells black and female Foreign Service officers they should file suit. Well, that rang pretty heavy on my ears. He just didn't want a Foreign Service that was all elitists. He wanted diversity. He wanted the Foreign Service to represent America. In 1996 Goodman, former associate dean at the Georgetown School of Foreign Service, wrote, "For a country regarded as the paramount leader in a multicultural world, the United States has yet to embrace its own diversity; continuing failure to do so will have profound consequences for governance." He has not changed. He continues to make impacts as president of the Institute of International Education, an independent, not-for-profit institution founded in 1919 that is among the world's largest and most experienced international education and training organizations. For more than forty years, it has managed the State Department's Fulbright Program.

Beginning in the 1970s, Alison Palmer and other Foreign Service officers won a series of class-action court orders that overturned discrimination against women in hiring and promotions. Yet only in 2010 did the State Department demonstrate that it was complying with court orders that included reparations to women and modifying hiring systems.

As a career counselor, I found it extremely difficult to encourage others to bid on Bahrain, Qatar, and other "garden spots" in the Bureau of Near Eastern Affairs because of constant Middle East conflicts and the lack of political and economic reform. I could not be disingenuous when I described these posts. They would be challenging, but they needed to be staffed. With 225 Foreign Service officers in my talent pool, 75 percent of them moved through the system during my two-year assignment. Most were stellar performers. One, Marjorie Ransom, was the first woman public affairs officer in Egypt. She was nominated to be ambassador to Yemen. Marjorie declined after the Senate Foreign Relations Committee held up her confirmation along with others for political reasons. I will never forget Tom Johnson. He went to Liberia when it was a very challenging assignment. Tom sent me a thank-you note for having presented his case before the assignment panel. He really wanted that assignment. Of course, when one person got his or her assignment and was satisfied, there were six to ten others who did not, and they were disappointed. Career counselors walked a fine line between being encouraging and honest at the same time. Fletcher's training proved valuable.

I was somewhat suspicious that the "system" encouraged African Americans to take African assignments. In principle, if the candidate had the qualifications, studied the language, knew the region, and had the appropriate earlier assignments, he or she was competitive. I was not the final arbiter for the assignments, but I had to represent each candidate based on his or her performance and not hue or corridor reputation. I carefully prepared for each assignment panel to ensure that each of my candidates received unbiased consideration.

There might have been colleagues who thought that, as a career counselor, I would set myself up for a "plum" assignment. That had been the assumption in the past, and I certainly did not wish to reinforce that assumption. Changing that commonly held perception, however, was not easy. So my next assignment, after a few glitches, might well have been perceived as a perk. My Abidjan mentor, Ambassador Stearns, unwittingly added to that perception. I am glad he reentered my career at this point.

After several invitations from Ambassador and Mrs. Stearns to attend dinner during Stearns's tenure as vice president of the National Defense University (1979–81), I reluctantly accepted. My reluctance was because I had attended so many command performance dinners while abroad, and I did not feel enthusiastic about attending what felt like another. I shudder at what might have happened to my career if I had not attended that dinner with Stearns's wife and mother. During the meal, he told me he was nominated to be the next ambassador to Greece. (He served as ambassador to Greece from August 1981 through September 1985.) He wanted me to be his cultural affairs officer. I was honored, but I told him the assignment system did not work that way. I would have to bid on the assignment. I also told him that others would perceive this posting as a very special assignment in Europe. Since I was a career counselor, others would assume I had used my position to get the assignment. He listened but still encouraged me to seek the assignment to Athens. I learned only in June 2013, at the fortieth anniversary of the Thursday Luncheon Group, that Ambassador Stearns called Roburt Dumas, then the director of the Foreign Service Personnel Office, to request that I receive serious consideration for the position in Athens.

At that dinner, I gazed at the artwork of the dining area, some of which included the Greek language. I thought to myself, this really looks foreign. I had not paid much attention to Greek letters since I pledged the Delta Sigma Theta sorority in 1962. I was sure I would not be able to learn this language. Ever the encouraging mentor, Stearns reminded me that my French was fluent and added that I could learn Greek. As we headed to the living area, I passed a series of Greek tourism posters and said to myself, Is he really serious? The Greek posters on the wall could have been hieroglyphics as far as I was concerned. Driving home, I reflected on the faith this ambassador had in me. By the time I parked the car, I had decided to bid on the Athens assignment.

Initially, I didn't get the assignment. Then Deidre Ryan, counselor of the USIA, a senior-level position I would take over in 1997, said it was a very difficult choice between Peter Synodis, an American of Greek descent, and me. Jim Hackett, then USIA's assistant secretary for administration, met with me. He suggested I go to Cameroon, which he described as the Switzerland of Africa. I told him I had served in sub-Saharan Africa, in Abidjan, Dakar, and Bamako. I also noted that when I lived in Paris, I made several trips to Switzerland. I had no desire to go to the Switzerland of Africa. Finally, I said I had served in Africa long enough and politely left his office. That was it. Hackett then sent a note back to personnel: "Find something good for Miss Elam; she's impressive." At that point such kind words were small comfort. I realized that he did not have to send that note, but now I am glad he did. Personnel made a genuine effort to find me a comparable assignment.

5

Harriet, How Is Your Greek?

If you talk to a man in a language he understands, that goes to his head. If you talk to him in his language, that goes to his heart. —NELSON MANDELA, South African statesman

I was taken by surprise one day by a call from one of my career counselor colleagues, Jack Tuohey: "Harriet, how is your Greek?" And, without giving me time to respond, he added, "You are going to Greece." He was serious. The assignments panel had selected me to succeed Peter Synodis in Athens as cultural affairs officer, also referred to as cultural attaché or CAO. A few months after my meeting with Jim Hackett, Synodis had moved from the cultural attaché job in Athens to the press attaché job, a post he had held in other countries. (Synodis died in September 2011.) I guess none of my career counselor colleagues dared inform me that I was being considered in case the committee did not approve the assignment.

Soon I was off to the Foreign Service Institute for a year of Greek-language training with five other students. Once again, I was the only African American in the class. Two of the students constantly made light of the training and did not appear serious about learning Greek. USIA was very strict when it came to language training. We were not allowed language waivers to go to a language-designated post. I was soberly aware I had to get the coveted 3 speaking and 3 reading proficiency levels. The scale is 1 to 5, with 3 considered the minimum level required to do the job in that language and 5 considered the same fluency as a highly educated native speaker. The language itself was difficult, and an added task was to master a different alphabet. The senior Greek teacher, Takis Sapountsis, said to me, "We want you to do well," then patted me on my shoulder. I bristled. He may not have known it, but from his body language and tone of voice, I sensed he was patronizing me. That was all that I needed to excel. From that day I was determined to pass my Greek examination. I was forty-two years old, and the synapses in my brain did not work as swiftly as they did when I was twenty-one. Yet I passed the Greek exam and earned the 3/3 level of reading, writing, and comprehending Greek. I felt pretty good about myself.

The assignment to Greece was my shining moment. My work, countering a daily diet of anti-Americanism, terrorism, assassinations, and political tension at the highest levels of government, proved to be significant. Greece had been under a dictatorship after a military-led overthrow of the democratic government in 1967. Former elected leaders lived in exile until democracy was restored in 1974. Election challenges and financial scandals had kept Greeks living under Cold War political tension and terrorism.

While I was in Athens, several Americans were killed by the Marxist guerrilla organization known as 17 November during a rash of kidnappings and killings that also included British nationals as well as high-profile Greek businessmen. Regional instability that included the 1974 Cyprus coup and Turkish invasion was followed by the 1981 Greek election of a left-leaning party with a neutral to anti-American platform. That backdrop made life difficult for all Americans posted in Athens.

As a result, the State Department's diplomatic security team flew to Athens to brief the entire embassy staff. They suggested we should not read or leave visible in our cars the *International Herald Tribune* or other English-language publications. Male employees were told not to wear the obvious American polyester slacks and other clothing easily identifiable as American. After I listened to the security officer for almost forty-five minutes, I raised my hand and asked, "And what do you suppose I do?" The briefer, a white American, recognizing my dilemma, responded, "I guess that's like asking me to take a low profile in Zambia." During my years in Athens, 1983–87, I did not have the braids I wear today. I suggested to him that I could cover my head with a scarf and speak French. Perhaps the terrorists might think I was from French-speaking West Africa or one of the former French colonies in the Caribbean such as Guadeloupe or Martinique. I was careful, but there wasn't much I could do. I was an American, a black American. In some respects, I thought I had little to worry about. All of the Americans who had been killed up to that point were white. Even during the hostage crisis in Iran, most of the women and minorities were released. That might have worked in my favor . . . at least until I got to Istanbul, Turkey, where an African American was targeted for attack. He survived the attack, but he was seriously injured.

Cold War politics kept Greece on edge during my tenure. Greece at that time was a "hardship" post because of the anti-Americanism. U.S. diplomats were allowed to curtail their activities because of the violence. During my last year in Greece, a bomb exploded under a passenger seat on a Trans World Airlines flight from Rome to Athens, killing four Americans. The pilot managed to save the remaining passengers and crew. Less than six months after my departure, Captain William Nordeen, the defense attaché, became the fourth American victim of 17 November. I had worked with Nordeen in Athens. I attended his memorial and burial at Arlington Cemetery.

Although Greek crowds demonstrated in front of our embassy once a week, we did not let that deter us from our work. We carried on diligently to raise America's profile and remove the host of misperceptions Greeks had about America.

For four years, nearly every Greek contact I invited to my events and programs attended, which, I was told, had not been the case with previous cultural attachés in Athens. Greeks invited me to their homes, many of whom were on the embassy's coveted A-list of contacts. I seized every opportunity to educate Greeks about African Americans in science, education, and technology. The audience for two of the Fulbright lectures I presented in Greek included members of the Greek Academy. Although initially intimidated when I learned of their presence, I got through the speeches. The Fulbright director, an American married to a Greek and fluent in the language, threatened to sit in the front row and make faces to keep me calm.

Just prior to my September 2005 retirement from the Foreign Service, I received word that I had been selected as the Dukakis fellow to teach for a month at the American College of Thessaloniki. What an honor, especially for someone from Massachusetts, to hold that position, named in honor of the former governor who appointed my brother to the Massachusetts Superior Court. I retired on September 30, and on October 10, I flew to Thessaloniki. What a joy to teach bright young Greek and American exchange students. They were well read and informed about international events. While there, I spoke to high school classes at Anatolia College and found them equally impressive. Once again, I saw the value of educational exchange programs. These young men and women, possessing an extraordinary level of global awareness, would one day become our leaders. This kind of interaction early in their lives gave them a favorable impression of America that would last a lifetime

I decided to visit Athens after the teaching assignment at the American College of Thessaloniki. My weeklong visit was a delightful trip of reunions with former contacts, who made me feel particularly welcomed. One of Greece's respected journalists, George Papastefanou, sent me a note that said, "When you and Ambassador Monty Stearns were here, we called it the Golden Age of Diplomacy." I shared that precious note with Ambassador and Mrs. Stearns.

I had learned on my first tour in Greece that the Greeks had a charming way of welcoming you into their orbit. I also learned they often had an ulterior motive. They were deep-thinking, serious, philosophical people, but they also thought that a letter of recommendation from the ambassador or cultural attaché could secure their son's entry to one of America's most prestigious universities. It was hard to convince Greeks that a letter from a U.S. government official would actually be counterproductive in our independent university system.

One of the key goals of an embassy's cultural office is to highlight the full spectrum of American arts: literature, all music genres, dance, painting, and sculpture. In one post I might host country-Western and bluegrass music, a few weeks later Chick Corea or Buddy Guy, and then the renowned Leonard Bernstein. I also coordinated the performances of the Dance Theatre of Harlem, the New York Ballet, the New York Philharmonic Orchestra, and Alvin Ailey's American Dance Theater. All of these groups performed in Athens during my four-year tour. The late Mstislav Rostropovich, one of the world's greatest cellists, standing next to me moments before his 1984 Athens Music Festival performance, told me, "Thank you for all of your efforts. I know that the cultural attachés do all the work to ensure a successful cultural event abroad." Ambassador Stearns heard this remark. I was absolutely thrilled by such an acknowledgment. It was a brief but powerfully sincere statement.

My access to and rapport with Greek government officials and members of academia was excellent. Unlike many of my other posts, Greece had a minister of education and a separate minister of culture. The film actress and political activist Melina Mercouri, who had been elected to the Greek Parliament in 1977, was the minister of culture. She epitomized Greece for many of my generation for her political activism and her acting roles in *Never on Sunday* (1960) and *Topkapi* (1964). My interaction with her began on a high note when she met me at the National Press Club in DC while I was studying Greek for the assignment. After someone introduced me as the new American cultural attaché in Athens, she commended me on my Greek and gave me her undivided attention in the midst of a room filled with folks far more important than I. Her riveting blue eyes fixed on me and made me feel as if I were the only person in the room. Her focus never wandered until we finished our conversation. That communication lesson has stayed with me throughout my career. Mercouri was not one of those who shook your hand and then clearly let you know she was looking for someone else in the crowd. While I was in Athens, Mercouri acknowledged me at each official event we attended. There were plenty of them. Granted, I had something called "high visibility." It was pretty hard to get lost in a crowd as an African American woman who happened to be the cultural attaché at the American embassy.

I accompanied Ambassador Stearns to see Melina Mercouri in preparation for the 1984 Olympics in Los Angeles. We were to confirm Greece's participation in the cultural aspects of the games in Los Angeles. All of us recognized that Mercouri was charismatic. I could not blame Ambassador Stearns, who with all of his dignity seemed totally enchanted listening to her. As she went to light her cigarette, the ambassador was at the ready to provide the match. After the amenities seemed to go on a bit too long, I felt obliged to interject with, "Excuse me, Mr. Ambassador; Washington is patiently awaiting details about Greece's artistic participation in the Olympic Games." We finally got down to business, but as I watched her, I could understand the ambassador's slight distraction.

If I were to highlight the most memorable activities and programs of my time in Greece, it would be our facilitation of a joint U.S.-Greek production of Euripides's *Medea* by the Boston Opera Company. In 1987 Sarah Caldwell, one of the first woman directors of an opera company in the United States, if not the first, came to Greece to inform the embassy and the Ministry of Culture of her plans for the Boston Opera Company's production of *Medea*. Caldwell wanted to use Greek opera singers, set designers, and other artisans who would make costumes from fabric woven in Greece. This task required close collaboration with Melina Mercouri. One could not find two more dramatic, highly expressive, and uncompromising women than these two. I often use my work with the two of them to illustrate the relationship of culture and politics.

Sarah Caldwell would call only a day or two in advance, saying she was headed to Athens for a meeting with Melina Mercouri. It never entered Caldwell's mind that a bit more advance notice might be helpful. Caldwell was an artist, and small details like preplanning are seldom a priority in the minds of creative people. Just prior to one of Caldwell's trips, the American military had carried out a major bombing campaign in Southeast Asia. The Greeks did not agree with our actions. I knew that the Caldwell-Mercouri meeting would be tense. As we entered the minister of culture's office, Melina said to Sarah, "I can barely speak with you today. Given your country's actions,

I may have to go out to the front lines and fight myself." Ever the dramatist, Melina's opening salvo came as no surprise to me. Sarah's matter-of-fact response was: "Madam, I didn't bomb anything. The U.S. government did." We made little headway during that meeting. In fact, Caldwell let me know that she considered she had made a very expensive trip from Boston to Athens for nothing. It was unproductive because of the American military's actions. Caldwell returned to Athens weeks later and had a productive meeting in a less tense atmosphere. If one thought politics, culture, and diplomacy are not entwined, this interaction proved they are.

Athens continued to provide me with professional challenges and lasting memories. As if the *Medea* production was not enough to keep me occupied, our section had another major project in 1987. We helped coordinate Greece's Archeological Museum and Washington's National Gallery exhibit entitled *The Human Figure in Early Greek Art.* The exhibit traveled throughout the United States for the next two years. Mercouri agreed to travel to Washington to open the exhibition, which drew nearly 260,000 people from January to June 1988 before traveling to Kansas City, Los Angeles, Chicago, and Boston. The Washington showing illustrated the value of excellent curators, who made each of the precious items shine in the settings in which they were placed. I had seen the same historic works in Athens, but the dramatic settings in the National Gallery were magnificent.

As I said earlier, Mercouri is an acting icon in Greece, and she is known throughout the world. She knew the powers of her charm, and she used it constantly. One of her greatest goals in life was to get the Elgin Marbles back to a museum at the Acropolis. The Greeks and the British have disputed ownership of this collection of classical Greek sculptures and other works of art, sometimes also called the Parthenon Marbles. Greek authorities have accused Thomas Bruce, the seventh Earl of Elgin, of looting the sculptures in the early 1800s when he was ambassador to the Ottoman court of the sultan in what today is Istanbul. The collection ended up at the British Museum in London after the British Parliament purchased it from Lord Elgin in 1816. Greece challenges the British position that the collection was legitimately acquired, contending that the Ottomans had been bribed and, in any case, as occupiers of Greece, had a dubious right to allow Lord Elgin to remove the treasures.

The late J. Carter Brown, the revered longtime curator of the National Gallery, joined Mercouri in a joint press conference just prior to the opening of *The Human Figure in Early Greek Art*. Mercouri had just taken the stage, and she wanted to put pressure on the British Parliament and bring an end to the long and tense negotiations for the return of the Elgin Marbles. The negotiations, long stalled, had nothing to do with U.S. policy. We counseled Mercouri not to mention the Elgin Marbles during the press conference, which was to focus solely on the exhibit.

But of course, she did mention them. Mercouri could not resist this golden opportunity to perform. After all, she is an actress who just happens to be from Greece, a country that loves drama. And the journalists ate that up. She knew they would run with that subject. We did not keep her from raising the issue of the Elgin Marbles. On the other hand, Brown was totally prepared for the press conference, and he gave more thoughtful answers to the press. His responses indicated he had studied the intricate details of Greek art. Although the press focused more on Mercouri's concern about the return of the Elgin Marbles than we would have preferred, Brown's erudite assessment of the collection made up for Mercouri's theatrics. The exhibit was a huge success.

Besides Mercouri's own political stances, her filmmaker husband's politics landed her on the Look Out list of people who required State Department approval before the embassy could issue her a visitor visa to enter the United States. I think she enjoyed it. Her husband, Jules Dassin, had been subjected to the anticommunist hysteria of Senator Joseph McCarthy and the House Un-American Activities Committee. The Hollywood blacklist of the late 1940s and into the late 1950s had put others in prison. Dassin left Hollywood and resumed his film career in Europe. In 1966, after her 1962 divorce from the wealthy landowner Panos Harokopos, Mercouri married Dassin. She starred in several of Dassin's films. He died in 2008. For the four years I was in Athens, whenever she was going to travel to the United States, we had to check with Washington before she was cleared to travel.

When I returned to Athens in 2005 after my time as the Dukakis lecturer at the American College of Thessaloniki, I rode the Athens Metro for the first time. I could not control my emotions when I arrived at the Acropolis Station, and there was a stunning shot of Melina Mercouri in front of the Acropolis. She had been given a state funeral after her death in 1994. All of my positive memories of interacting with this iconic figure in Greek culture came back. I shed a few tears. She was absolutely marvelous in life, and her legacy continues to this day.

My return to Greece also refreshed my memory of another high point of my previous time in Greece, the successful negotiations for the television production rights for an American dance troupe's performances to appear on Greek television. Ambassador Stearns's successor, Robert Keeley, asked me to work with the Dance Theatre of Harlem's director to re-telecast throughout Greece its performances at the Odeon of Herodus Atticus, the ancient stone amphitheater at the base of the Acropolis. This task was given to me because of the heightened anti-Americanism in Greece at that time. Keeley thought that this respected representative of American culture would help improve America's image in Greece. After tense negotiations in Greek with the Greek impresario and the dance theater's founder and executive director, Arthur Mitchell, we reduced the original fee from $100,000 to $40,000. Even more important, we persuaded the Greeks to pay these fees in U.S. currency, rather than Greek drachma, as they originally proposed.

Ambassador Keeley, who had openly expressed the need for more positive images of the United States because Greeks remained highly skeptical about America, was pleased. He noted fewer sharp criticisms and even some positive observations about America from Greeks in areas away from Athens. The performances were televised throughout the summer, and the Greek press covered them. They really appeared to soften the strident press coverage the United States had received.

Modern dance took on the role of the diplomat. I found it doubly satisfying that a predominantly African American dance company helped improve the U.S. image in Greece. Workshops, master classes, and social events cemented the Americans' relationships with fellow Greek dancers.

Once, while I was walking down the streets of Athens with members of the Dance Theatre of Harlem, Greeks thought I was a dancer, too. Was I thrilled! How I wish I could have been Judith Jamison, but heaven knows I was not. I tried to improve my posture the entire time I was in their presence. We can all dream, can't we?

I did get my chance to take the stage. I played the role of Dominique Devereaux (Diahann Carroll's role) in *Dynasty* at Athens College. Ambassador Stearns had a cameo appearance as Blake Carrington's majordomo, Joseph Arlington Anders, whose loyalty to his longtime employer made him suspicious of Carrington's new bride, Linda Evans's Krystle, played by the ambassador's wife, Toni. Canadian John Summerskill, president of Athens College, played Blake Carrington. Toni recently recalled that her husband's thirty seconds on stage and his one line, "Carrington residence," when he answered the phone was marred by a glitch. The phone never rang. Afterward Toni told him that he should have turned to the audience and said, "A good butler always knows when the phone is about to ring."

During rehearsals, I thought I would never get the role down. I just did not feel comfortable being that kind of mean character on the stage. As we came closer to the performance time, I had given up on trying to be the word that rhymes with "witch." I stormed off the stage, saying, "I am not doing this. I'm just not an actress, and I cannot be the royal b—— [I didn't say the word] that I'm supposed to be in this role." Well, everyone at that rehearsal clapped, and Michael Kakoyiannis, one of Greece's foremost directors, said, "That's just what we wanted. That was great!" Another lesson learned! I got even louder applause the night of the performance. However, that was my last attempt to be an actress.

Some might consider Rome or Paris as the prime posts for cultural attachés, but let me assure everyone, Athens was equally exciting. At that time, there were reports that there were more theatres in Athens than on Broadway. I often attended two or three exhibit openings or plays each week. The setting was fertile ground for cultural diplomacy, and we capitalized on that fact while I was there.

The American embassy's Cultural Section mounted one of USIA's blockbuster exhibits, *The History of Filmmaking in America*. We transformed the Greek National Gallery to resemble a traditional marquee of a Hollywood theater. To land such an exhibit in Athens was unprecedented. Again, it was Mercouri's charm that persuaded the former USIA director, Charlie Wick, now deceased, to send this exhibit to Greece. We learned that Mercouri had discussed her interest in having such an exhibit with Wick at an international culture conference in Mexico. Such a blockbuster exhibit was designated for Eastern European countries. There was a line item in the budget for exhibits to be sent only to countries behind the Iron Curtain. During the Cold War, USIA exhibits were particularly important in such regions to provide another view of America to those constantly exposed to communist propaganda.

The filmmaking exhibit incorporated artifacts, costumes, music, and props from internationally recognized American films. Wherever the exhibit was shown, we tried to ensure that one of the original actors or composers who won an Oscar would exhibit the statuette. A few years earlier, the Greek composer Vangelis, who wrote the music for *Chariots of Fire*, had agreed to allow his Oscar to be exhibited. When our chief exhibit director brought the Oscar to my office, he mentioned he would take it back to London, where Vangelis resided. I quickly stated that, as the culture attaché in Athens responsible for the mounting of this exhibit, I would gladly take the Oscar back to London and hand deliver it to Vangelis. Honestly, I don't know where I got the nerve to say that, but I did. Once the exhibit closed, I took the Oscar to London. I had managed to catch a horrendous cold just prior to the trip, but I was determined to go. Filled with all sorts of antihistamines, I arrived at Vangelis's residence and delivered the Oscar. His living room was filled with his instruments and synthesizers. I thought to myself, this is a total wreck, and what a shame this stunning classical living room is filled with all of these electronic instruments. Then I realized, this is his life, his workshop, and I stopped being so judgmental. Vangelis was most cordial. We discussed the concerns we both had about a young Greek opera singer I had discovered, Markella Hatziano. Her agent was overly demanding. Vangelis knew him and knew of Markella, and he gave me important guidance to share with Markella upon my return to Athens. Markella now resides with her family in Nebraska and continues to perform in the United States.

In Athens I became fast friends with Margaret Murphy of Santa Barbara, California, who was in the Consulate Section, which issues visas and helps American citizens with problems abroad. For me, as a Bostonian, Margaret's name suggested she should be red haired, freckled, and Irish. Everyone in Athens just assumed I knew her. We met after I had been there almost three months. That's when it dawned on me why people assumed we knew each other. She wasn't red haired and freckled. She was African American. Although from two very different parts of the United States and with very different backgrounds, we became close friends and traveled together around Europe. After my brother Clarence died in 1985, I needed to get away. Margaret and I went to Morocco to clear my head. While we were in Morocco, we visited all the famous places. We rented a car and hired a retired USAID driver. He drove us throughout Morocco, including Casablanca, Fez, and Marrakesh. At one of the stops, I was bitten on my thigh by a yellow jacket or some other stinging bug. Now, most people who know me as Miss Priss could not imagine I would drop my Bermuda shorts in the back of the car with this male driver, but this sting hurt. The driver dashed down to get some saltwater to make a mudpack for me to put on it. Well, by this time, Margaret was in hysterics. I didn't care who saw me. This sting hurt like the dickens and was swelling up. The driver was very discreet. He never looked my way, he just sort of handed the mudpack to me. It took the sting out.

Whenever we traveled, Margaret did the bargaining. She enjoyed it. In one instance, while we were in Morocco, Margaret had just changed currency to be able to shop in the marketplace. While at one shop, Margaret looked at me and asked if I had any other Moroccan dinars, to which I was supposed to answer no. That would help her in negotiating a lower price. Instead I said, "But Margaret, you just changed some money." Honestly, if looks could kill, I would not be here to share this experience with you. (As if I had not learned my lesson, when we went to a large indoor fabric market in Hong Kong, I spotted a piece of fabric I really liked. I said in a not-very-subtle voice, "Margaret, I like that, in fact, that's exactly what I've been look-ing for." Margaret gave me that look again and responded, "Now that you've told the world you liked that fabric, don't expect me to bargain for it. The sellers already know you want it, and I doubt that I'll get it for a good price.")

Once, when our bill came after a dinner at an elegant Moroccan restaurant, we were both taken aback a bit at what we thought was the price. The amount was written with a comma, not a decimal point, as in the United States. Shocked at what we thought was a $200 meal, we gave a tip calculated on that amount. The waiter was so very honest and returned with so much change, we looked at one another. When he explained that the bill was only twenty dollars, we had to smile at one another. That's what happens when you try to be a sophisticated traveler and you really are not. We were far more careful reading bills from then on.

Midway through my time in Greece, my nephew Jay, who had completed his bachelor's degree at Harvard, earned his doctorate of dramatic arts from the University of California at Berkeley. Jay (Harry J. Elam Jr.) was promoted in January 2017 to vice president for the arts as well as associate vice provost for undergraduate education at Stanford. This man with all the titles is now very much like his dad, always well dressed at Stanford. That was evident when I flew out to Stanford last May to surprise him for his sixtieth birthday.

What better reward for an aunt to give someone graduating with a doctorate in drama than a trip to Greece? Knowing I could not show favoritism, I also invited my niece Winifred, the daughter of my oldest brother, Charles.

Colleagues thought that my "little niece and nephew" would be coming to visit, not adults. The first day after Jay and Winifred arrived, I was thrilled to be able to treat them to a Greek comedy performed at the site of one of Athens's many ancient ruins. *Lysistrata*, by Aristophanes, is a comic account of one woman's extraordinary mission to end the Peloponnesian War. Lysistrata persuades the women of Greece to withhold sexual privileges from their husbands and lovers as a means of forcing the men to negotiate peace—a strategy, however, that inflames the battle between the sexes. The opening scene begins with a significant display of phallic symbols. Lo and behold, here I thought I was being the consummate host by giving Jay and Winifred almost front-row seats to the performance. I was seated about five rows behind them. I was mortified when I realized that Winifred, with her very conservative nature, might not find the humor in any of this. It was too late. I suffered until the intermission, when I was able to explain the symbolism. After all, the play was in classical Greek and she (as most of us) had no idea what the dialogue was about. I gained yet another life lesson in terms of welcoming travelers from abroad. Provide them with every bit of background before taking them to a cultural event. I should have at least given her a synopsis of the play in English. Jay and I had to chuckle. Of all my nieces, Winifred was the least likely to find such a play enjoyable. Oh well, onward and upward.

I did much better as a host to Winifred when she came to Turkey. She was hesitant about visiting Ephesus. When I reminded her of the biblical significance of this famous site and that she would be following in the steps of St. Paul in his travels, she quickly changed her mind.

Now Jay has become a big man on campus at Stanford, but then he had a few things to learn, especially how to dress when one visits a U.S. embassy. After an outing on a hot day, Jay and Winifred could not get a taxi to return to the embassy, so I went down to the center of Athens to pick them up. As we pulled into the embassy parking lot, I said to Jay, "Now you can put on your shirt." Jay responded, "This is my shirt!" Well, it was a tank top that resembled the sleeveless undershirts my father used to wear. Although that might have been in vogue at that time, it was not appropriate attire when entering a U.S. embassy. I suggested that he amuse himself walking around the neighborhood until I finished work in about an hour. He did.

My sister, Annetta Elam Capdeville, and her husband, Andrew, also visited Athens. Andrew was blind, but one day I took him for the entire day to "see" areas near Athens. I was hoarse and mentally tired by day's end. I had to describe every scene and every item in one of the museums. My sister's role for thirty-three years was to be Andrew's eyes, and doing it for just one day wore me out. She never complained.

Andrew regaled my Greek colleagues with his commentary on their flight to Athens. When the flight attendant accompanied him to the restroom entrance, she mentioned that the light would come on when the door was closed. He reminded her not to worry, that he would not need the light. He was known for many self-deprecating comments and delightful humor. My colleagues marveled at how he comported himself at the dinner table. Once you told him where his food was located on his plate (using a clock face as his guide), he had no problem enjoying his meal. Often you forgot he was legally blind. When I visited with them in Denver during my sister's early stages of Alzheimer's, I marveled at how Andrew made certain their home was a safe environment.

The 1982 television show *Fame* was probably one of the most positive things we could export, rather than *Dallas* and *Dynasty*, because the show was based on an existing school of performing arts in New York. The show focused on academic excellence as well as the performing arts, and both are hard work. The young characters were allowed to perform only if they met their academic requirements. That positive approach to the arts was a welcome relief from the attitudes portrayed on some other American television programs. Debbie Allen played the role of dance teacher Lydia Grant. The show opens with her telling her students, "You've got big dreams? You want fame? Well, fame costs. And right here is where you start paying . . . in sweat."

Allen came to Athens to put on choreography workshops. She was five or six months pregnant with her son. (She is married to former

NBA player Norm Nixon. Their son, Ellard Nixon Jr., played college basketball and became an actor.) She was talented, and she danced as part of the workshops. At one point we took her to another city on the outskirts of Athens, and she had some discomfort. Her doctor put a stop to the workshops. But what concerned me was the fact that she, like a lot of artists, thought that because the U.S. government was covering the costs, she could have all the comforts of first-class accommodations. She was somewhat demanding and didn't quite understand the limits of the expenditures allowed at the Athens Hilton Hotel. It fell to me to give her the "come to Aunt Harriet" talk, explaining that this was taxpayer money. She was not the only artist who presented me with that issue. I learned from that experience to brief all performing artists ahead of time on the limits—they could not order champagne, wine, and other extras just because they were here as the guest of the Department of State. Yet another lesson to be learned, which was not part of any of my courses on diplomacy. I had become the stern Aunt Harriet and not "the little Elam girl."

When I served in Athens, I had the joy of going often to Thessaloniki, a beautiful and ancient city in northern Greece. In 1983 I attended an international basketball competition where none other than the legendary Dean Smith and his North Carolina team were playing Greek, Yugoslav, Italian, and a number of other European teams. After three games that stretched late into the night, I represented the U.S. embassy as the cultural attaché at a dinner for the American team. I recall Coach Smith giving a touching blessing. But the dinner, the awards, and the speeches lasted until well after midnight. I was getting sleepy while seated at the head table. I decided I might wake up if I walked around. I wandered over to the table where the North Carolina team was seated. I saw this young man who turned out to be Michael Jordan seated with his parents and some of the Yugoslav team members. They were all carrying on. They didn't speak the same languages, but somehow they were communicating. I was fascinated. As I sat there and watched them interact, I saw the value of sports diplomacy and of sports in bridging cultural and political gaps.

When I felt someone's foot under the table, I was a bit concerned, thinking someone was playing footsie with me. Not at all. It was one of the players two seats across the table from me, but his legs were so long they reached my end of the table. I got so tickled that I woke up, and was able to go back to the head table to finish the rest of the evening. What we do for God and country!

Earlier that evening I had the pleasure of meeting then–NBA commissioner David Stern, who was seated with my Thessaloniki friends Roula and Pandelis Dedes. Pandelis, now deceased, was a lawyer in northern Greece who specializes in sports law, and he loved basketball. Once again, the friendship established with them in Greece has lasted to this day. Roula and Pandelis visited me in Senegal, where they seemed to absorb as much as they could of Senegalese art and traditions. I particularly enjoyed entertaining my European guests in Senegal. They seemed to have a greater interest in the traditions and culture of the country than in purchasing souvenirs, which all too often was the main focus of American tourists.

I was in Thessaloniki again to welcome Chick Corea, the legendary jazz pianist and composer. While sitting at a table I saw a nice glass of what I thought was water, and I was so thirsty that I gulped it down. It was straight ouzo, and my esophagus lit up. I learned from that experience not to assume that just because something is very clear and in a glass, it is water. I should have taken note that the glass was much smaller than a conventional water glass.

While in Thessaloniki for another speaking engagement, I gave a talk on African Americans in science and technology to the Fulbright Alumni Association in northern Greece. Now, ordinarily that would not have been unusual, but I gave the entire address in Greek. This decision, as hard as it was, was probably why I became so warmly received and remembered in Greece, both in Athens and Thessaloniki. Despite the work required to give that speech, I agreed, when asked, to deliver it again in Athens to another packed audience. A member of the Greek Academy was present and came to express his appreciation for my sharing in his native language this valuable information about America. The positive coverage in the Greek and English press confirmed the value of my effort.

At the end of my four years in Greece, my brother Harry came to help me celebrate at events held in my honor. He was thrilled to bask in the glory of his little sister. I knew he wanted to come because he gave up a planned trip to Disney World with his grandson. That told me I had fully gained his respect. My father was no longer living, which made my brother's esteem that much more meaningful. That was something I wanted. Harry was the person who knew Greek and Latin. He could read the quotes at museums in ancient Greek.

At one of the going-away celebrations, Harry joined the men in a traditional Sirtaki dance. The Greek men thought he was amazing. So did I.

During my four years in Athens, I received what I thought were excellent evaluation reports. Just before the promotion list was to be published (by worldwide telegram), one selection panel member (long deceased) made a cardinal error. He called to tell me I was on the promotion list before the list was published. That is never to be done. To this day, I do not understand why this officer thought he should break that rule. When the official list was distributed, I could not find my name on it. My heart sank. I wanted to believe there was a serious error. Having since served on several selection panels, I know strict regulations require the panel to forward a list of the top-scoring candidates for promotion. However, the final list depends on the budget available at the time. There is no guarantee everyone on the list will be promoted. Panelists are now required to take oaths of secrecy to eliminate such problems. After that devastating experience in the mid-1980s, I was terribly disappointed. I wanted to resign from the USIA. Fortunately, a dear friend, now deceased, Ofield Dukes, counseled me to remain and to continue to excel.

I spent four years in Greece without a promotion. Perhaps I was so engaged in moving Greeks away from their anti-American tendencies, I did not realize that my boss, the public affairs officer (PAO), might have perceived my actions as threatening to his role in the embassy. He noted in his evaluations of my performance, "She was so well received that they thought she was the PAO." In my naïveté, I thought this was a compliment. Later, thanks to the counsel I received from the then–deputy director general of the Foreign Service and later ambassador William Swing, I found out that such comments and other less substantive observations added nothing to my evaluation and, in fact, were detrimental. Although the PAO included significant commentary on the political situation in Greece, he did not mention the specific actions I took, including negotiating a huge reduction in television rights to telecast the Dance Theatre of Harlem's performances countrywide, persuading the National Gallery of Greece to be the host for a blockbuster U.S. exhibit, and organizing other educational and media-related programs that reduced the anti-Americanism fervor prevalent in Greece in the late 1980s. In my innocence, I thought the references to Greece's political situation were sufficient. I did not realize that specific examples of my work to ease anti-American stances were critical. William Swing provided me with the encouragement I needed to craft more specific examples of my accomplishments in my subsequent evaluations to ensure I got credit for my work. Swing, who later served as ambassador to Liberia, is now the head of the UN International Organization for Migration. He is one of the rare FSOs with six ambassadorships to his credit: People's Republic of the Congo, Liberia, South Africa, Nigeria, Haiti, and the Democratic Republic of the Congo.

Despite the absence of a promotion, I had four absolutely wonderful years in Athens, probably the most exciting time of my career. Even today I believe the Athens assignment gave me more personal satisfaction than being an ambassador. It was the interaction with musicians, academics, journalists, and artists like the Alvin Ailey Dance Company, the New York Philharmonic, Leonard Bernstein, cellist Mstislav Rostropovich, the Dance Theatre of Harlem, Twyla Tharp, Pilobolus Dance Theater, Joan Myers Brown, Buddy Guy, Herbie Hancock, and Wynton Marsalis, to name a few, that made it so exciting. I sipped ouzo with Chick Corea in northern Greece. I dated a cellist and a Greek theater director for quite a while. I experienced cultures that little girl from Boston never imagined.

6

The Desk Officer Who
Was Never in Her Office

It struck me that these black women were a unique group. The modern women's movement hadn't taken place yet, and they achieved these things at a time when the country was in turmoil. The country was not extending a hand, not saying, "Gee, we want you to come and show us your gifts and what you have to offer to us," either because they were black or because they were women.
—PHOTOGRAPHER GERALD FRASER, 1989, on his portraits in a Vanguard exhibit, *I Dream a World*

After Greece, I came back to be a USIA country affairs officer for Greece, Turkey, and Cyprus. Also referred to as the desk officer, this officer analyzes incoming reporting on the countries noted. The desk officer also supports administrative and program requests from the field, briefs outgoing delegations to those countries, and provides an oral report during the weekly geographic area director meetings. Once again, I was the only person who looked like me in the weekly State Department meetings in the Bureau of South Eastern European Affairs.

Even though I had been a career FSO for several years, most people in Washington assumed that a woman was a staff aide, a secretary, or an administrative officer. In those days, most male career FSOs appeared to have minimal respect for the support staff who laid the groundwork for the high-minded negotiations they would conduct. After all, they were the so-called substantive officers. Anyone else was administrative support staff and of less consequence than they were. Sadly, some of these officers would appear not to recognize me when walking in the corridor or on the street outside of the State Department Building. I could sense their surprise when I offered my in-depth brief on Greece, Turkey, and Cyprus. USIA desk officers often carried the portfolio of two or three countries. State desk officers handled only one. From my perspective, their jobs were much easier.

As if Greek politics were not complex enough, the Greek prime minister, Andreas Papandreou, was having an affair with Dimitri Liana, who became his third wife after his 1981 divorce from American-born Margaret Chant Papandreou. As I reported on the protracted conflicts with Cyprus and Turkey, I had to include less political but often more curious reactions to the prime minister's affair with a former talk-show hostess and flight attendant half his age.

Unlike some of my State colleagues, I visited all my Turkish posts: Istanbul, Ankara, Smyrna, and Ephesus. I met with the ministers of education and culture in Cyprus. USIA European Bureau (EU) desk officers could not travel to their countries, for the majority of the area's budget had been depleted because Director Charles Z. Wick had used the new and expensive Concorde jet to fly to his meetings in Europe. As a result, minimal funds were left for EU desk officers to travel. I used my frequent flyer miles to visit my countries. USIA covered my per diem, and off I went. The visits were invaluable. This face-to-face exposure confirmed to me that, despite their strained relationships, Greece, Turkey, and Cyprus had much in common. The public affairs officer in Turkey and I developed a respectful working relationship during that visit. I listened to his concerns about his staff. In his evaluation, he indicated the post felt they had an advocate in Washington.

Whenever I got a PAO request for increased budget funding or when a time-sensitive response was needed, I personally went and met with the appropriate officer in the governing bureau. Unlike my other colleagues, I did not send a memo (today it would probably be an email request). Instead, I hand carried the request and engaged my colleagues in conversation. I worked the corridors to get my posts what they needed. Written memos tend to sit in an inbox until the crisis erupts. I knew it was harder to deny a request if the person making the request was sitting in front of you. I became known as the desk officer who was never in her office.

I have noted that some new and old diplomats tend to dismiss the support staff in embassies. I remind new Pickering Fellows, outstanding individuals from all ethnic, racial, and social backgrounds, that it is very important to respect the support staffers, logistic staffers, dispatchers, and drivers. They will not be able to make a policy démarche if they do not have a car that works to get them to the appropriate host-country ministry. This brings to mind my relationship with the executive director of USIA's European Bureau, Jim Gavigan. He became one of my closest colleagues. After my return from being ambassador to Senegal, Jim sent me an email and suggested that I return to active service because my management style was needed. As flattered as was, I had no desire to return to the department. Serving as an ambassador was the highlight of my career.

My next assignment, to Turkey, was a direct result of my work as the desk officer for Greece, Turkey, and Cyprus. My first visit to Istanbul as the desk officer broadened my knowledge of a fascinating country and culture. During that trip I met with Consul General William "Bill" Rau and had lengthy conversations with him about his career. He noted he had served in Greece before coming to Turkey. I said to myself, if Bill could learn Greek and Turkish, perhaps I could. After all, I had tackled Greek and its alphabet. Turkish is written in the Roman alphabet. That gave me the false impression that Turkish would be easier. I was absolutely wrong. Turkish was the most challenging language I have learned. The syntax and sentence structure were, in my view, totally convoluted. I found it more complex than German or Latin. The verb is at the end of a sentence; instead of saying, "I'm going to the store to buy a loaf of bread," in Turkish your sentence is somewhat like, "Store loaf of bread to buy going I am." And if you put an adjective in there, it gets really dicey. Turkish is an agglutinative language, which means you add a suffix to the word to complete that word's meaning. In essence, you could have one word with fifteen different suffixes and that would constitute a sentence. Wrapping my mind around that at age forty-seven was a task.

I completed half of a nearly yearlong FSI language-training program. Some classmates did not appear as though they took the course seriously. I requested that USIA enroll me in one of the other language schools we used when FSI classes were full. Fortunately, I had a wonderful teacher for the next six months of study. It was not easy, but I was motivated by the teacher's patience with me. I learned Turkish.

My motivation to pass the Turkish exam came in June 1990 when I sat in the gallery as Nelson Mandela spoke to a joint session of the U.S. Congress. That event was two weeks before my final Turkish exam. I used every contact I had so that I could attend that speech. Mandela was awe inspiring. I told myself if he could spend twenty-seven and a half years in prison and not be bitter, I could pass my Turkish exam. For the next two weeks I closeted myself and studied. Mandela spoke on June 26. I passed my Turkish exam on July 5.

Mandela continues to inspire me. Earlier in my career, I declined a South African posting during the apartheid era. During the trip I made in 1998 as USIA's counselor and acting deputy director, I met a wide spectrum of South African educators, leaders, and entrepreneurs. While serving as U.S. ambassador in Dakar, I opened an art exhibit in 2001 entitled *Places in Our Lives*. The exhibit illustrated the role of artists in diplomacy. The artists represented a full range of the ethnic groups that compose the United States and shape the human mosaic from which our nation derives its greatest strength. The exhibit included Howardena Pindell's *Mandela's Parade 2*, which captures the spirit of those I met in South Africa. People expressed unbridled enthusiasm, anticipation, and joy whenever the recently freed Mandela visited a city, town, or village.

I have written that Athens was my shining moment. Well, that was before I spent four marvelous years in Istanbul, Turkey. Istanbul is the cultural and business center of the country, much as New York is for the United States. I was the U.S. branch public affairs officer in Istanbul, a city larger than the capital, Ankara, the site of the U.S. embassy. If a review of our embassy staffers' daily calendars of meetings and events were not enough to confirm the vibrancy of Istanbul, the monthly visits of our ambassador, first Robert Strausz-Hupé and later Morton Abramowitz, ended any speculation as to which city was more dynamic. As I said, Istanbul reminded all of our visitors of New York City.

Ankara had historical museums and was the seat of government, but Istanbul offered multiple venues for performing artists, exhibits, and conferences. But I also knew I dared not alienate my Ankara colleagues, especially since they controlled the size of my budget. Whenever I proposed a program, I made sure to include a stop in Ankara. My speakers and my performing artists might not have wanted to go to Ankara, but I made sure that they were part of that mix.

Work in Istanbul brought a few stimulating challenges. Hours prior to Secretary of State Warren Christopher's arrival in Istanbul for one of the NATO ministerial meetings, I received a call from the press officer on his aircraft. Christopher wanted to host a lunch for the traveling press once he arrived in Istanbul. He knew his relationship with them was strained. The secretary's venue of choice was a luncheon at the Topkapi Palace Museum. And he wanted to serve Bloody Marys. As often is the case, in vino veritas, one speaks truth with a bit of wine. Without a second thought, I said we could work that out. I immediately called the senior cultural assistant, Meral Selcuk, to see if it might be possible. Working entirely from home, she gained permission to use a dining room in the palace. She confirmed the Topkapi waitstaff would be dressed in period costumes. When I mentioned that the secretary wished to serve Bloody Marys during the lunch, Meral paused, then admitted that might be a problem. The palace is located across the street from a mosque. Alcohol is not served in buildings or restaurants with close proximity to a mosque. Since I was occupied with other details for the press corps visit, I left this event in Meral's capable hands. Lo and behold, when I looked out of the window of the Topkapi Palace, I noted Meral walking with a spritely gait to the palace with two red picnic jugs in her hands. I guessed what was in them, and I was right. She had mixed the Bloody Marys herself. Readers of this work who have served in Turkey and know Meral Selcuk will not be surprised. Meral is considered one of

Turkey's national treasures by all American diplomats who have been fortunate enough to work under her tutelage in Istanbul.

Mike McCurry was the State Department spokesman during Secretary Christopher's tenure. He noticed that even in the pouring rain, Turkish staff at the hotel waited for the American secretary of state to arrive and depart. He made a point of holding up the press bus to take time to thank the kitchen staff and waitstaff. He also thanked all of my press staff for their work during the visit. I have not seen another press spokesman do that. I was truly impressed.

Istanbul had some rocky moments, too. After attending a performance of Mozart's *The Abduction from the Seraglio*, I was walking with Melvin Wittler, an American protestant missionary in Turkey from 1956 to 1993. Our cars were parked next to each other. My driver spotted something hanging from Wittler's car. That was the first time I came that close to death. The bomb would have seriously, if not fatally, injured all who were close to it. Mel Wittler and I were already good friends, but we became even closer friends after that.

Mel's papers were given to the Yale Divinity School Library upon his death in 2003. He was in Turkey under the auspices of the American Board of Commissioners for Foreign Missions and the United Church Board for World Ministries. They published what is considered the most reliable English-Turkish dictionary. The dictionary is still sold on Amazon and is entitled *Redhouse English-Turkish Dictionary*. The Dev Sol Turkish Terrorist group bombed the offices of Redhouse Publishing Company on January 21, 1991.

Americans were not loved around the world. Events in Istanbul, like events in Athens, reminded me to remain conscious of my security. The night we found the bomb on Mel's car, I spent about two hours on my knees. Over and over again I said, "God, I promise I will do the right thing from now on. Mama and Daddy, I love you, but I'm not ready to see you quite yet."

When George H. W. Bush came to Turkey in 1991, the consulate went into the usual advance preparation mode. For six weeks, we had daily countdown meetings with the advance team. One member of the advance team was one of the people who worked closely with political consultant Roger Ailes, the creator of the infamous "revolving door" negative television ad used against Michael Dukakis. Along with the Willie Horton "Weekend Passes" advertisement, it is considered to be a prime factor in Bush's defeat of Dukakis. The ad was produced by Ailes with help from Lee Atwater and first aired on October 5, 1988. "Revolving door syndrome" is a term used in criminology to refer to recidivism; however, in the ad the implication was that prison sentences are much too short. You can imagine my reaction when I learned that one of the advance team members had worked closely with Ailes on this ad. I knew, however, that our task was to ensure a successful presidential visit. I put aside all of my angst about the negative ad, which sadly today might seem mild in terms of presidential campaign ads that have followed, and went to work. Public servants serve the people we elect as well and faithfully as we possibly can, no matter the party.

We drafted, edited, cataloged, and filed scores of briefing papers for the traveling press and coordinated the complex arrangements for the pressroom at the Conrad Hotel in Istanbul. There were no cell phones or digital communications. The now old-fashioned modems had to be installed. Istanbul might have reminded us of New York, but the infrastructure and lack of availability of state-of-the-art technology (e.g., fast copying machines) made it plain we were not in New York City.

Appealing photo ops are always essential to presidential and secretary of state visits. Global audiences are more likely to focus on the photo than the news coverage of the visit. President George H. W. Bush is six feet, two inches tall, and the late Turkish president, Turgut Özal, was significantly shorter. We arranged for a riser for the Turkish president to stand on when photographed with President Bush at the Hagia Sophia and at the Blue Mosque so both presidents conveyed the stately look all heads of state try to project.

On the same presidential visit, embassy staffers were tasked to shuttle videocassettes from each site visit to the pressroom at the Conrad Hotel for swift transmittal to American media (network and cable) outlets. We had what we thought was a foolproof schedule. Somehow, after one stop I discovered the videocassette was left behind. I quickly grabbed it and dashed at my best speed to catch up with the lead cars, handing it to the next designated person in what resembled a relay race. Like most women, I love pretty shoes, but I knew pretty was not a consideration for that day. I knew to wear flat, rubber-soled, comfortable shoes. Thinking back on that experience, I am sure my colleagues would get a charge out of seeing "the branch PAO in Istanbul" dashing along the motorcade to do the handoff.

At the end of a state visit, embassy and consulate staff are not allowed to leave until the president's plane takes off safely and is out of sight. Traditionally, one of the pool reporters joins the staff on this "Death Watch." Once the plane is safely in the air, the "wheels up" party begins. In this case we kicked off our shoes and proceeded to unwind in the elegant Cirigan Hotel, which overlooks the Bosporus, where the presidential party stayed. This former palace built for an Ottoman sultan in the 1860s was restored, enlarged, and converted into a five-star Kempinski hotel. After further renovations in 2007, it resembles an authentic palace. We had a grand time in that stunning setting. On my subsequent visits to Istanbul, I often reminisce about that "wheels up" party. It tops many similar parties I have experienced in other overseas posts, primarily because of the hotel's elegance and ornate style.

In Turkey, I found that even a small dinner took just the right timing and diplomacy to work. It took me two years, but Ambassador Richard Clark Barkley was pleased when I arranged his dinner meeting with the eminent Turkish scholar Ekmeleddin İhsanoğlu, director of the Islamic Research Center, the foremost research center on Islamic history, and Sami Kohen, the revered journalist at the *Milliyet* newspaper and the most influential Jewish journalist born in Turkey.

I invested a lot of time to secure this dinner engagement for the American ambassador. I had to develop a rapport with each of his potential guests before I could suggest it. After all, why would one Jew and one Muslim want to sit down with an American just because I wanted it to happen? I had to approach it in a way that almost made them think they suggested it. I also had to sit at the dinner and be ready to write a memorandum for the State Department about it. All three of the dinner participants left with far more positive, less skeptical views of one another. I cannot remember the reporting cable we sent back to Washington, but this initial meeting led to easier contact and dialogue with key opinion leaders in Turkey. One of them, İhsanoğlu, ran for president of Turkey in the 2014 elections.

In my diplomacy course at the University of Central Florida, I emphasize the importance of building genuine relationships in order to be an effective diplomat. While I was in Turkey, I became close friends with Orhan and Candan Fetvaci. He managed a commodities trading firm, and she ran a philanthropic foundation. They had two girls in private school. Zeynep Fetvaci was fifteen years old when she insisted on interviewing me at my Istanbul apartment. Her topic for a school paper was women in the diplomatic service. Recently, she shared her memories of that day: "I was extremely nervous as I was very much in awe of you, and I wanted to make a good impression. I'm not sure if you remember, but I was thinking of studying international relations early on, and you were the main reason behind that. I wanted to be like you one day! I guess I have steered away a little (well a lot probably), but I still hope that one day I can be viewed as an amazing, interesting, compassionate, and elegant lady as you are!" Now, some twenty years later, she works in the London office of a New York–based real estate firm that raises capital for private equity real estate firms around the world.

Zeynep's sister, Emine, then sixteen, has graduated from two well-known U.S. universities, Williams College and Harvard, earning her PhD in history of art and architecture, focusing on Islamic art. During one of my visits to Istanbul, her mother handed me a huge book, Emine's doctoral dissertation, and said, "This book is my grandchild." I smiled and said, "Be patient." A few years later I attended Emine's wedding in Istanbul. Now a professor at Boston University, she has published a color-illustrated book, *Picturing History at the Ottoman Court*. Her husband, Dan, originally from Australia, is in the Philosophy Department, teaching courses on ethics. They have an eighteen-month-old daughter and the predictable doting grandparents in Turkey and Australia. Emine Fetvaci attended my brother Harry's funeral in Boston in August 2012, as did Ambassador and Mrs. Monteagle Stearns. Oh how thoughtful! Her presence touched the very core of my being. Emine did not know my brother. This little girl from Istanbul and her sister have grown into fine women. I feel particularly fortunate to have maintained contact with them over the past twenty years.

A description of my assignment to Turkey would not be complete without mention of a photography exhibit we mounted in Istanbul and in Izmir. *I Dream a World: Portraits of Black Women Who Changed America* presented a very positive perspective about America that the world needed to see. Brian Lanker, a white photographer who won a Pulitzer Prize for newspaper feature photography in 1974, had taken 225 pictures of women of color who had made significant impacts on the lives of others, from the well-known, including Barbara Jordan and Rosa Parks, to the unknown, including Priscilla Williams, his children's nanny.

The actual exhibit included some seventy-five photographs. Each photograph highlighted a positive interaction between black and white Americans at a time when such relationships were not common. I first viewed the exhibit at the Corcoran Gallery in Washington DC. Immediately, I knew our international audiences should be exposed to it. I knew a number of senior officers who respected my judgment. I told them they should see the exhibit. Once they saw it, they agreed it was worth sending the exhibit abroad.

The Turks came to the exhibit opening, which for a host of reasons beyond my control, was held the very night of the beginning of Ramadan. To ensure a decent turnout, I knew I had to do something special. To demonstrate my genuine respect for their presence that evening and their culture, I gave all of my remarks in Turkish. Ambassador Richard Barkley traveled from Ankara for the event, and he gave his remarks in English. I thanked our Turkish guests for spending the first hours of the first night of Ramadan with us at the exhibit opening. We secured a prime location in the center of "downtown" Istanbul. The gallery was filled. The following day, even the seasoned Istanbul cultural staffers were impressed with the positive press coverage of the opening. The seldom-highlighted story of African American women who played pivotal roles in civil rights, the arts, and education opened the minds and hearts of Istanbul's intelligentsia. The Turks were genuinely fascinated by this history. For three weeks, middle school teachers brought their students, and university and technical schools also sent students. During the exhibit, we hosted two U.S.-based speakers who gave further insight into the historical relevance of these women in American culture.

My ultimate accomplishment in Istanbul involved international politics. An article appeared in one of Turkey's fundamentalist newspapers implying that the United States had been supplying food and weapons to Kurdish terrorists known as the PKK. Ambassador Morton Abramowitz instructed me to meet with the newspaper's editor to clarify this misinformation. Rather than blindside the editor, I told him the subject of my meeting, so that he could be prepared. I went with all the Washington-provided facts on disinformation campaigns in the region. I outlined how this disinformation was used in press articles, including the one that brought me to the meeting. With my senior Turkish press assistant, Bertan Saracoglu, we conducted the entire meeting in Turkish. The next day, the paper ran an apology. Bertan said it was the first time in the thirty years he had worked at the American consulate that an apology was published.

We also presented an American studies conference on works by African American writers. The Turkish English professors knew far more about Toni Morrison than I did. As part of this conference, USIA sent U.S. lecturers to discuss and analyze the images of Americans of color as portrayed in literature or in the media. I took the opportunity to tell the gathering about the professional careers of my family, including five lawyers, a judge, teachers, published authors, and now a vice president at Stanford University. I added that the majority of my nieces and nephews had attended college: Yale, Princeton, Harvard, Lincoln University, Tufts, Johnson C. Smith, Duke,

Radcliffe, and Vassar. Many African American families are just like mine, I explained. Some have far more impressive accomplishments and positions.

These two overseas assignments, in Greece and Turkey, geographically close but very different and both demanding, required me to master new languages, to immerse myself in their fascinating cultures and navigate around old conflicts in a most subtle and effective manner. The religions are different, but Greece and Turkey have a long history of a constant attachment. Forward-thinking leaders from both countries, including Mustafa Kemal Atatürk of Turkey and Eleftherios Venizelos of Greece, were strong proponents of mutual understanding and agreement. At the time of this writing, there was an attempt to move the two nations closer to one another and to put aside the conflicts that have existed throughout the past twenty-five years. I saw the change when I went back to Greece and Turkey in October and November 2006. The earthquakes that took place in the late 1990s in Turkey and in Greece brought those two countries together, because they had to help one another to survive those natural disasters. In these tragedies the people took to heart God's message of love and reconciliation to jointly overcome adversity and build better relations between their two nations. Yet, with the Greek economic crisis and Turkey drifting toward dictatorship, I am not able to paint such a rosy picture of Greek-Turkish relations now.

The experience of being the cultural attaché would have been heady for anybody, but for someone who grew up going to museums in Boston kicking and screaming, I find it ironic that I ended up thriving in a position as U.S. cultural attaché. I went to cultural events as a child and teenager on the orders of my brothers. It truly was not free will. After I came home from postings in Athens and Istanbul, I went to a Kennedy Center performance of *Les Miserables*. I did not have to go backstage and make sure the sound system was right. I did not have to write a telegram saying how the audience reacted to these American performing artists and whether any U.S. objectives were met. I could just sit and enjoy, which I did. I know my brothers are smiling in heaven.

7

Well, It's the Truth!

American traditions and the American ethic require us to be truthful, but the most important reason is that truth is the best propaganda and lies are the worst. To be persuasive we must be believable; to be believable we must be credible; to be credible we must be truthful. It is as simple as that.—EDWARD R. MURROW, director of USIA, during a 1963 congressional hearing

My assignments in Greece and Turkey provided me with a deep swing through the cradle of civilization. My role was a dual one: to articulate U.S. policy and to correct the many misperceptions about the United States through educational and cultural exchange. At times, I was a teacher. Afterward, I became a student, a student of my own country. I was one of a select group of FSOs and potential flag military officers chosen to attend the State Department's Senior Seminar for the 1994 academic year.

I had applied for the Senior Seminar, but I had no response until Jeffrey Lite, then director of USIA personnel, informed me that an ambassador in Turkey was very much impressed with me. That ambassador was Richard Barkley, who succeeded Ambassador Morton Abramowitz. Ambassador Barkley was concerned that I had not received an ongoing assignment as my time in Istanbul drew to a close. He called USIA Personnel to check the status of my Senior Seminar application. Jeffrey Lite told Barkley he had not seen my application. At Barkley's strong suggestion, I faxed all of the materials again, and shortly afterward I became a member of the thirty-seventh Senior Seminar. I spent an academic year learning how domestic policy impacts foreign policy. I accompanied my seminar classmates to such iconic sites as the former World Trade Center in New York, the Chicago Board of Trade, the New York Stock Exchange, and CNN headquarters in Atlanta. We met with Americans from all walks of life. We traveled to the poorest parish in Louisiana, to Little Havana and Little Haiti in Florida, and to the North American Aerospace Defense Command (NORAD), the combined organization of the United States and Canada that provides aerospace warning, air sovereignty, and defense for northern America out of Colorado Springs. We also received briefings at the atomic testing ground at Sandia Laboratories in Albuquerque, New Mexico.

My twenty-nine colleagues in the Senior Seminar, the Department of State's most prestigious program for diplomats identified as having promising futures, included six women and three African Americans. Two of the African Americans, Robert Perry and I, became ambassadors. Robert Perry served in the Central African Republic. The other African American, Keith Brown, became USAID's deputy administrator for Africa. The class included the current (2017) ambassador to Russia, John Tefft, who was our class president. I was vice president. Several other classmates became ambassadors, including Barbara Bodine to Yemen, Elizabeth Raspolic to Ghana, and Ellen Shippy to Swaziland. A few of the six military officers became generals. But one of my closest military colleagues is one I least suspected would become a friend.

I will admit that I am most uncomfortable with southern accents, no doubt because of my generation's close ties to those who suffered under the overt segregation of Jim Crow in the South. For years, anyone with a southern drawl was not likely to get much of my attention. That changed when I met Marine colonel Mark Adams during the Senior Seminar. He did not fit my stereotyped image of white southern men as narrow-minded racists. He was from Arkansas, and, as I learned, he had no interest in interacting with people of color as he grew up. Upon his arrival at college, much to his disbelief, his math professor was an African American woman. Yet when we traveled throughout the South, he did not seem to mind being seated with me and the two other black members of the Senior Seminar. His involvement with the Promise Keepers movement added to his credibility. Popular in the mid-1990s, the Promise Keepers promoted reconciliation among men from different racial, socioeconomic, and denominational backgrounds.

Our time together helped both of us dispel racial stereotypes. Years later, Colonel Adams and I worked together to establish a minesweeping program in Guinea-Bissau, the nation on Senegal's southern border where mines caused a tragic loss of lives. Once again, building personal relationships with colleagues proved invaluable.

As part of the Senior Seminar, we toured the USS *Enterprise*, now retired from service but the world's first nuclear-powered aircraft carrier. The ship, at 1,123 feet, remains the world's longest naval vessel. It is a huge ship, employing forty-six hundred service members. I hoped it would look big from the air because we had to land and take off from the carrier while it was in motion. At Newport News, Virginia, we boarded a military transport aircraft for the flight to the aircraft carrier. Looking around for someone experienced in these matters, I took a seat inside next to Army Colonel Bob James. Once we were strapped in tight, I learned it would be his first landing on an aircraft carrier, too. The takeoff went like so many other commercial flights I had taken. However, upon our lightning-like descent to the carrier, I could not breathe. The plane stopped on a dime. I had similar trepidation about the slingshot takeoff when we departed. True enough, the carrier's catapults snapped the plane into flight speed, and it just seemed to go straight up. Although I dare not repeat that exercise at my current age, I found it exhilarating after we landed safely on our return to terra firma in Virginia. I have the greatest respect for our navy and the rest of our military. Bob James remains in touch. He is at a military academy, where he teaches and prepares students for potential careers in international affairs.

Our travels included visits to all the branches of the military. The psychological impact of military training was new to me and to many of the civilians in the course. Colonel Adams's presentations on the training of young Marines was riveting. Without a doubt, the Marines go through the toughest training. It is extremely hard on the recruits. I naïvely questioned a commander about what seemed to be abuse by the training officers in southern California. "No one asked them to join the Marines" was his straightforward reply. If I had not considered it before, I now realized that these Marines were training to be the first on the ground in a time of crisis and were trained to kill people, not to make judgments. That was a very sobering realization.

During the seminar, I learned one does not rely solely on the bid list to determine future assignments. I learned that State officers (unlike USIA officers) lobbied for their assignments. As I sat in our conference rooms between sessions, I listened to several officers calling area directors to convince them that their qualifications made them the optimum candidates for positions or assignments. At first I listened in disbelief. Self-promotion seemed so crass. However, that was the accepted practice at State, and officers who were not proactive did not get the career-enhancing assignments. I do not say the "better" assignments, for career-enhancing assignments often mean going to a hardship post or a war zone.

Our class president, John Tefft, was confirmed as ambassador to Russia in July 2014. John encouraged me to seek the public affairs counselor position in Brussels. I was reluctant to contact the European area director for State. John made the necessary first call. The next thing I knew, I got word from the USIA European area director that I should definitely bid on the PAO Brussels position. I did. The ambassador was a political appointee, Alan Blinken, an investment banker from New York. At first, Blinken insisted that I travel to Brussels for an interview. After all, he was used to the corporate approach. The U.S. government was not going to fly me to Brussels for an interview, and I wasn't keen on using my frequent flier miles for such travel. Finally, the sitting PAO, Ashley Wills, convinced Blinken that I did not need to come to Brussels and that I was capable of handling the post. (Ashley was U.S. ambassador to Sri Lanka in 2000–2003.) The assignment was confirmed, and I went to Brussels in early August 1995. I appreciated Ashley running interference on my behalf.

A quintessential international city, Brussels provided me with a much-needed window on the complexities of multilateral diplomacy. It is the site of the European Union headquarters, and the NATO mission is only forty minutes from the capital. Most nations have representatives accredited to the European mission, to NATO, and to Belgium. In essence, most nations have three ambassadors assigned to Belgium at the same time. During my two-year Brussels tour, all three U.S. ambassadors were political appointees. Stuart E. Eizenstat was the U.S. ambassador to the European Union. Robert Hunter was the U.S. ambassador to the U.S. Mission to NATO. Alan Blinken, as the U.S. ambassador to Belgium, was considered first among equals. Imagine all three of these high-powered and highly political individuals serving at the same time in a medium-sized European city. Predictably, they often ran into one another at official events. I enjoyed watching their interactions.

I met with Ambassador Blinken a few hours after I arrived in Brussels. He offered a warm welcome and was not at all intimidating. At that point, though, I would never have predicted that we would stay in touch over the past twenty years. The assignment proved to be mutually beneficial.

However, the first substantive issue the ambassador raised started off with his comment, "We are probably going to get some flack in the press tomorrow because of my comments about the Vlaams Blok party." In response to a journalist's question about the right-wing, nationalist party gaining popular Flemish support, the ambassador had answered, "I could never vote for a party that held such extremist views in any country." The view in many parts of the Belgian community was that the Vlaams Blok was racist. One of the senior Belgian ministers implied the party did not include all ethnic groups in Belgium. Although Blinken did not make that statement, it would not be difficult for the media to imply that meaning given public opinion at that time. I cringed as I thought about the repercussions, and I quickly let the ambassador know it was not the most discreet statement to make. Blinken responded, "Well, it's the truth!"

What a welcome! My first day on the job (and as probably the first African American PAO in Brussels), and already I had to smooth over comments by the ambassador that a Belgian opposition party was packed with extremists. What did I do to deserve this? I told the ambassador that he should ignore anything that might appear in the press. Sure enough, the next day a news article quoting Blinken appeared. We said nothing, and the story disappeared from the media.

However, the days that followed the ambassador's comment brought positive responses from the Belgian prime minister, the foreign minister, and even the palace. As I reminisced with Ambassador Blinken in preparation for this work, Blinken told me he received a phone call from the Royal Palace indicating a "certain gentleman" agreed with what Blinken had said about the party. The ambassador said he could not get firm confirmation that the comment was from the king of Belgium, but that was the assumption.

After a trial in 2004, Belgium banned the Vlaams Blok party as racist. Some of its members restructured the party under a new name, but Belgium's other political parties have united to exclude the new party from joining coalition governments.

That introduction prepared me to expect the unexpected from a successful Wall Street banker.

Blinken often told me and other senior embassy colleagues that it seemed the U.S. government could find all sorts of reasons for not doing things. In the private sector, Blinken's work environment included a large staff of savvy corporate lawyers who found legal ways to get things done. Blinken told three of us who served on his country team, "When I propose an idea or a project, I want you to find a way to get it done, but legally." Trust me, all three of us understood our marching orders, and we did precisely that. Terence Flannery, the foreign commercial service counselor; Lange Schermerhorn, the deputy chief of mission; and I worked closely together during those two years to launch most of the ambassador's realistic projects.

One of the first proposals, and the most successful, was to establish a Trade and Investment Information Center for the newly independent states of the former Soviet Union. International entrepreneurs visited Brussels frequently. Many were from the newly independent states. They needed access to information about business laws and potential clients without having to make long-distance trips. A trip to Brussels was more convenient and economical than a trip to the United States. Blinken instinctively knew this center would heighten the profile of the U.S. embassy in Brussels. He was absolutely right.

Blinken's engaging personality helped. He would eat lunch in the embassy cafeteria, chat with visiting family members, and even permit photo opportunities. I had never encountered an ambassador who would frequently lunch in the cafeteria. The family members were in awe. They could return to their stateside homes and say they met the ambassador. I have the utmost respect and admiration for my former career ambassadors, but Blinken provided me with the template to be approachable and engaging when I became an ambassador.

One experience in Brussels showed me that the U.S. military sure knows how to do ceremonies and left a lasting impression. Few ceremonies could match the swearing in of an ambassador, but somehow the uniforms, brass, and music at military ceremonies were exciting. In June 1996 I met a young army second lieutenant at a promotion ceremony at Supreme Headquarters Allied Powers Europe Brussels. As I listened to this highly articulate voice read the president's "proclamation" for a recently promoted lieutenant colonel, I asked a friend to introduce me to the speaker. His name is Frank Walker, now a lieutenant colonel and the inspector general at Fort Meade, Maryland. More important than titles, however, he is a genuinely caring human being.

Several months after I met Frank at that ceremony and after a few other discussions, I learned he was a golfer. My big brother, Judge Harry Elam, and his wife, Barbara, were coming to Brussels. My brother loved golf, and I set up a golf game with Frank. Frank, then the most junior officer in his detachment, recalls asking his boss for a day off and casually mentioning his plans to play a few rounds of golf. What was first met with ridicule and scorn took a dramatic turn when Frank mentioned his golfing partners were the chief justice of the Boston Municipal Court and the judge's sister, the public affairs counselor at the embassy. Suddenly his "boondoggle" had become an "outing," with arrangements made by a lieutenant colonel, a master sergeant, and for good measure, an additional captain. Frank was grilled on his knowledge of golfing rules and etiquette. His trusty 1982 Opel Ascona was deemed unacceptable transportation. Instead, the chief justice would ride in a gleaming new Peugeot 406. After eighteen holes, Frank found himself before a quickly convened, ad hoc All High Supreme Military Golfing Council, where he reported that the judge's golf game was just as sharp as his superior legal mind. That was almost twenty years ago. Yet, after hundreds of rounds of golf since that day, Frank recently wrote, "That one round with The Judge has been the only one that has ever required a full military debrief at its conclusion. In the end, it was worth it all. The Judge was a gentleman and a noble soul—generous with his wisdom and incredibly gracious. I am a better man (and a bit of a better golfer) for having met him."

Frank spent a recent Mother's Day with me along with his wife and golden retriever. When his mother passed away a few years after I met him, he asked if I would be his adopted mother. I was moved to tears when he made that request. Although I have more than enough nieces and nephews whom I love dearly, Frank is the son I never had. Wilfred has warmly welcomed Frank into our lives. I thoroughly enjoy watching the two of them banter. They bring much joy into my life.

Through an extraordinary tip of fate, three of the top U.S. embassy Brussels posts were held by women: the deputy chief of mission, the deputy defense attaché, and the public affairs counselor, me. When Madeleine Albright was named secretary of state, we were ecstatic. We called the ambassador and informed him we were headed to his office to celebrate. He had the champagne waiting. A longtime friend of Madeleine Albright, he could not have been happier. Once we finished celebrating, it was back to work for each of us.

I would estimate that it rained in Brussels 300 out of the 365 days a year. I remember commending one of my colleagues for her excellent tan in the midst of the constant rain. She said she had to go to Florida on her own "R&R" to get some sun. I told her I'd better book myself on a similar flight, for if the rain continued, I risked losing my permanent tan.

If I thought the rain and cool temperatures in Brussels were draining, I was in for a rude awakening when I left that international city to spend the Christmas holidays in the French Alps with my French family. Off I went to the scenic, but cold, ski resort–like setting in the mountains. Although I am from Boston, I had never before slept with a heated brick in my bed to keep warm. Other than a winter visit to our embassy in Ottawa, I cannot remember ever being so cold. While sporting my winter coat and several layers of clothing, I played a word game to distract me from how uncomfortable I felt. It did not work.

After a day in the cold, I faced a cold bed. By the second and third days, my body became acclimated to my surroundings. Once again the warmth of my French hosts helped me forget about the temperature. I am so glad I made that trip in 1997. Mme Marthe Sassard died just a few years later, in 2003.

NATO ministerial meetings took place once or twice a year in Brussels. That meant we could count on visits from the U.S. secretary of state and the foreign ministers of NATO-member nations. My colleague Marc Grossman, who would become U.S. ambassador to Turkey (1995–97), assistant secretary of state for European affairs, and undersecretary of state for political affairs and who succeeded Richard Holbrooke as the U.S. envoy to Afghanistan-Pakistan, would call to alert me to a visit by the secretary of state. He sometimes made light about the heady task of managing the motorcade from the airport to NATO meeting sites. Usually the U.S. ambassador to the country is the only person who accompanies the secretary from the airport. In Brussels, Marc had to determine which of the three ambassadors would ride with Secretary of State Warren Christopher from the airport to the hotel. Having three high-profile ambassadors, each with his own agenda and each with a desire for private time with the secretary, made that choice difficult. I remember suggesting to Marc that he have the transport officer set up a relay. Have one ambassador ride with Christopher for one leg of the trip, another the second leg, and the third would be on the final leg of the trip.

The U.S. ambassador to Belgium was first among equals. My relationship with the public affairs officers was similar. At one point during my tour, all three were women. My signature was required for all post budget requests sent to USIA Washington. The three of us knew our respective portfolios, and we did not thwart one another's work. All of us were committed to meeting the respective goals and requirements. We collaborated well.

The Brussels assignment gave me the first opportunity to work at a post with a binational Fulbright Commission. The commission in Belgium also coordinated the Fulbright Program in Luxembourg, which meant I had the opportunity to visit our Luxembourg embassy twice while in Brussels. Meeting with respected academics and businesspeople from both countries added to my excitement in working in a European post.

Ambassador Blinken enjoyed giving speeches, which meant I did a lot of speech writing. I worked doubly hard on drafts for Blinken. As I told him, I did not possess the southern humor of my predecessor, Ashley Wills. Blinken connected with his audiences, and I wanted to ensure he continued to do that in each draft I presented to him. To help me do that, he would stop in my office on his way to the residence—which was connected to the embassy chancery building—and he would sit down to give me his ideas on the messages he wanted to convey. My dear mother's insistence on my learning shorthand proved invaluable once again. I jotted notes as he outlined his thoughts. This was Blinken's operating style. It made my task much easier.

The time approached for the annual Marine Ball, and yes, another speech. I researched all I could about the ball and found a couple of appropriate anecdotes I thought Blinken would like. I practiced the delivery of some comical segments to see how they would sound to the audience.

I arrived at the Marine Ball in my "one best," as Mary Dougherty called her evening dresses. I was taken to my seat at the ambassador's table. I felt pretty special. The moment arrived for the ambassador to take the podium. Elegantly attired as always, Blinken walked to the podium, said a few words, and then threw up the cards with "my" speech! Yet as he launched into his remarks, he incorporated every one of the points I made, with just the right sprinklings of humor. He was a hit. The attendees loved his remarks. I was relieved. When he returned to the table, I leaned toward him and said, "Thank you for being the master communicator." I continued to carefully observe the ambassador during his briefings. He listened, asked for clarification when necessary, and absorbed the crux of the issues. He was a businessman who became a diplomat, a political appointee who did not take himself too seriously. He acknowledged the gaps in his foreign policy expertise and sought counsel from his career officers. His respect for the work of the U.S. Information Agency and the Foreign Commercial Service in establishing the Trade and Investment Center put those two agency heads on solid ground with him. That was not always the case in other embassies. We had our own budgets, and we were able to implement his ideas with minimal bureaucratic battles.

When Ambassador Blinken got word that Lange Schermerhorn, his deputy chief of mission, had been nominated to be ambassador to Djibouti, he called the entire staff to an impromptu reception to celebrate. The Blinkens hosted the country team members for holiday dinners and presented us with appropriate mementos to mark the occasion. Career officers do not have a budget for such "luxuries" or for "team-building activities." I had never been invited to an ambassador's residence other than for strict representational functions. This outreach was totally unexpected and, from my perspective, much appreciated.

In many ways Blinken had the management skills that some career diplomats do not possess. Being a foreign policy wonk is impressive, critical, and commendable, but one certainly needs a loyal team to support the ambassador at any embassy. Some staffers were not sure they liked his approach, but in the final analysis Blinken and his country team got the job done. He valued our work. How refreshing.

Months after we left Brussels, the labor attaché and I were honored to be included in Mrs. Blinken's birthday celebration at the Fairfax Hotel in Washington. There are not many ambassadors, career or political, who remember former embassy staff that way and invite them to a personal event.

Blinken also retains close ties with Belgians. In the past twenty years, the Blinkens have frequently traveled to Brussels. Further proof of Blinken's genuine rapport with the Belgians is his membership on the board of directors of a Belgian company and his continued ties to businessmen and sportsmen. The Blinkens attended my wedding, my swearing in as an ambassador, and my seventieth birthday party. My husband and I have been the Blinkens' guests at dinner either at their home or at another venue whenever our New York visits have coincided with their presence. We were pleased to have lunch at their residence in early June 2014.

Blinken's opening comment about the Vlaams Blok to me that first day—"Well, it's the truth!"—remains one of the positive memories of my time in Brussels. It is so rare in today's climate that leaders are willing to acknowledge facts and openly state what is a proven truth.

8

This Was Our "Aha" Moment

Public diplomacy...deals with the influence of public attitudes on the formation and execution of foreign policies. It encompasses dimensions of international relations beyond traditional diplomacy; the cultivation by governments of public opinion in other countries; the interaction of private groups and interests in one country with those whose job is communication, as between diplomats and foreign correspondents; and the processes of intercultural communications.
—EDMUND GULLION, who coined the term *public diplomacy* in 1965

In early July 1997, USIA director Joseph Duffey called me in Brussels and asked me to return to USIA as counselor. It was the USIA's most senior management position, but I would be the last counselor. I was flabbergasted. In two years the agency was slated to become part of the Department of State. Exchange programs and other USIA components would fall under the direction of the department's new undersecretary of state for public diplomacy and public affairs. I was fully aware that my USIA colleagues were justifiably concerned about the assimilation of USIA's mission into the Department of State and that the transition would be painfully uncomfortable. I could not believe Duffey wanted me to take on that task.

Once I agreed, I received a call from Assistant Secretary for Management Patrick Kennedy, who seemed almost too enthusiastic as he congratulated me on my new assignment. I was skeptical, but I appreciated his reference to my being a consensus builder. Pat Kennedy and I had collaborated on the colocation issue of USIA offices in embassy buildings in the past. We were always cordial in our discussions, despite USIA's heightened concerns of restricted access to foreign publics that came with colocation in embassy buildings. Standalone USIA foreign operations welcomed the public, whereas heavy security around embassies made visiting difficult. We made accommodations both agencies accepted. USIA and State, however, were two very different organizations, with two very different cultures.

To be effective advocates for U.S. government positions abroad, Edward R. Murrow, the first USIA director, said the agency needed to be present "at the takeoff," when policy decisions were being made, not just at the landing. Too often, however, USIA public affairs counselors were tasked with advocating for policies with minimal advance briefs and little to no contributions.

This "merger" was not going to be easy. I made every effort to select the most knowledgeable and objective USIA officers to coordinate with State on personnel, budget, and regional and functional bureaus. I researched the successes and failures of major corporate mergers. Since I was recovering from major surgery shortly after receiving my new assignment, I had time to do the research while I was in Brussels. The effort proved beneficial in my initial exchanges with State colleagues. None of us at USIA were pleased with the merger. Brian Atwood, the director of USAID, fought hard against the amalgamation, but USIA director Duffey did not contest it. The loss of a forty-year institution with a track record of success in building relationships in the global community remains a bitter subject among many former USIA officers.

Think tanks and academic institutions have written scores of studies examining the pros and cons of this merger, and many chronicle the value of USIA programs in the world's conflict regions. Others identify the need for educational and cultural exchanges that were the lifeblood of effective public diplomacy during the Cold War. I would venture to say, they are still the lifeblood of diplomacy in today's terror-filled world.

Imagine sixty-six hundred anxious USIA employees tasked with new responsibilities in the State Department, where the relationship was already strained. Distrust, dislike, and in some cases disdain filled the atmosphere. Pat Kennedy and I traveled to several regional public affairs officers' conferences abroad to be totally transparent on programmatic, administrative, and personnel operations once the merger was complete. Our candid discussions with embassy staffers at these meetings diminished much of the apprehension, but not all.

To mesh the staffs of the two agencies with minimal disruption was stressful, to put it mildly. I managed with the incredible help of USIA's senior policy officer, superb area directors, and dedicated administrative officers, including Kenton Keith, ambassador to Qatar, 1992–95. Miller Crouch, Steve Chaplin, Rick Ruth, Stan Silverman, and a host of colleagues provided realistic recommendations and comprehensive briefs on each aspect of the integration. In the majority of integration issues, their dedication to excellence and openness brought mutually acceptable results.

The politics inside USIA and in the Department of State made the Greek and Turkish conflicts I dealt with for seventeen years pale in comparison. The absence of reorganization legislation, continued budget cuts, requests for details from the State Department and other U.S. government agencies, ambassadorial and deputy chief of mission assignments, and frequent inquiries from Congress gave me daily opportunities to exhibit the conflict resolution skills I learned while at Fletcher. They also gave me ample opportunity to call upon the consensus-building skills that I gained from my Greek and Turkish assignments.

My daily interactions involved meeting with senior leaders in the Department of State, many of whom were political appointees. When I returned to USIA, my senior collaborators were career Foreign and Civil Service officers. Each group had a different perspective on the merger. Consequently, my approach to State was designed to provide immediate solutions while my USIA colleagues took a long-term view of the merger's effects on USIA programs. It was harder to change the mind-sets and perceptions of the career USIA officers than those of my new colleagues at State. For State officers, policy formulation was critical. How USIA articulated or promoted that policy was secondary. Few at State considered early policy deliberations with USIA area directors worth their time. Faced once again with the takeoff-versus-landing analogy, I attended each meeting armed with the best evidence to illustrate the importance of USIA officers being present when policy decisions were made. We would have welcomed being present when the George H. W. Bush administration contemplated the war in Iraq, when we could have presented approaches to developing messages for foreign audiences more likely to open dialogues with the United States, no matter how unpopular our actions might be in the affected regions.

Very few State officers understood the strategic planning involved before USIA mounted a cultural or educational event in a county. We conducted public opinion poll research before we crafted a new program. Before the detailed discussions that we held during the transition period, I am not sure many of our State officers realized how valuable such advance research could be for influencing and promoting the success of a policy initiative. When State colleagues became aware of the detailed work involved in mounting public diplomacy programs, they became far more interested in our approach.

Although the expression *public diplomacy* had existed since the mid-1960s, the term did not really take hold until the transition of USIA into the State Department. *Public diplomacy* was coined in 1965 by Dean Edmund Gullion at my alma mater, the Fletcher School of Law and Diplomacy. It deals with the influence of foreign public attitudes on the formation and execution of our foreign policies. It encompasses the dimensions of international relations beyond traditional diplomacy, such as the cultivation by governments of public support for their policies in other countries; interaction of private groups and interests in one country with those of another; local media reporting on foreign affairs and its impact on policy implementation; communication between those whose job is communication, as between diplomats and foreign correspondents; and the process of intercultural communications.

In the State Department there were four specialty career tracks for Foreign Service officers: political officers, economic officers, consular officers, and management officers. During the transition discussions, we established a new career track for Foreign Service officers entitled public diplomacy. A deputy assistant secretary for public diplomacy was designated for each geographic bureau. These geographic bureaus are responsible for directing what ambassadors do at our embassies and what priorities they embrace in every country where we have an embassy. Getting public diplomacy directly involved in this structure was our "aha" moment.

I found it enlightening. I attended State Department senior meetings four days a week, which Deputy Secretary of State Strobe Talbott and Ambassador Thomas Pickering chaired. They often gave me a bemused look when I spoke about public opinion research or press analyses in conflict regions. They probably expected superficial reporting from me on speaker or performing artist programs. I remember early on in my USIA career the reactions of some State colleagues who indicated they saw minimal value in a speaker or a performing arts program. Yet many of them were anxious to have their top contacts get tickets for such events. What better way to develop a relationship with a valuable contact than through social events and cultural outreach?

To this day, there is a misperception that public diplomacy is synonymous with public relations. Many political appointees, because they come from the private sector, often think that the terms are interchangeable. This misunderstanding has led to attempts at "branding" embassies and "marketing" America. Charlotte Beers, undersecretary of state for public diplomacy and public affairs, was convinced the Madison Avenue marketing approach would win friends and influence people, but America and its values are not products to be marketed. They involve complex institutions and belief systems that cannot be explained in sixty-second commercials. Advertising is not the right strategy for effective public diplomacy programs.

Meetings with State's senior leadership allowed me to highlight the value of speaker programs, ethics in journalism workshops, rule of law seminars, panels on civil society and women in government or entrepreneurship, and the all-encompassing American studies conferences. As I offered summaries of field reports that spoke of more positive U.S. press coverage, comprehensive political reports, and heightened credibility with contacts, I could see a change in State's view of USIA's work. Joseph Nye coined the term *soft power* in the late 1980s, but it took on greater meaning in the twenty-first century, especially since the 9/11 tragedy. For years, my USIA colleagues and I knew that our work was based on this concept. Soft power is considered the ability of a country to influence others to do what it wants through persuasion instead of force or coercion. We hear it frequently in foreign policy debates. We heard it often in former secretary of state Hillary Clinton's testimony before foreign relations committees. In fact, she might be credited with coining the term *smart power* as a combination of soft and hard power.

The more I read in preparation for teaching my UCF students, the more I saw multiple references to public diplomacy successes in the State Department and the Department of Defense. For example, U.S.–North Korean relations warmed up, albeit briefly, when the normally anti-American regime allowed the 2008 performance of the New York Philharmonic at a Pyongyang theater along with a broadcast of the concert on North Korean television.

For two tense years, I worked closely with my State colleagues to put in place a viable new structure within the department. My strongest and most trusted advocate in this process at State was Ambassador Marc Grossman. Marc and I had served together in Turkey in the early 1990s. We developed a positive working relationship from that assignment, which lasted throughout the rest of my diplomatic career. Whenever I had a particularly challenging issue, I would seek Marc's counsel. He appreciated USIA's programs throughout his career, and I was comfortable requesting his counsel.

Some bureaus in the State Department integrated USIA's officers directly into their activities. Other bureaus were less interested. The more skeptical State employees accepted the new former USIA colleagues as long as those officers did not compete with them for advancement. I was reminded of my arrival at State from the White House.

Miller Crouch suggested that we begin with USIA's Western European director, Brian Carlson. Not only did Brian possess the right temperament, but he was one of the most highly respected area directors in USIA. Brian worked with Marc Grossman to have an area director for public diplomacy housed in State's geographic bureau and help craft public diplomacy programs for the regions. That approach became the model for other bureaus to follow. It was a success mainly because of Marc's and Brian's intellects and personalities and their mutual respect. Having State and USIA staffers working in concert ensured well-targeted programs. USIA officers were at the "takeoff."

During the consolidation and with the steady support of my deputy Mark Jacobs, we wanted to ensure the viability of our respected training program. State agreed that USIA had an efficient training program for new, midlevel, and senor USIA officers. That integration went smoothly, no doubt because of the personalities of Dr. Katherine Lee, our director of training, and Ambassador Ruth A. Davis, then director of the Foreign Service Institute. USIA required a month-long course for press and cultural attachés to learn the historical and cultural landscapes of their new assignments. They arrived at post confident and prepared to navigate their new surroundings. Former USIA officers continue to teach effective public diplomacy courses at the FSI.

With area directors gradually becoming integrated in the State geographic bureaus, with our training program well integrated, and with the personnel systems moving toward total integration, a new undersecretary was announced. Evelyn Lieberman became the first undersecretary of public diplomacy and public affairs after the consolidation. She came on board a few months before the formal ceremony took place. Lieberman, Secretary Albright, and I presided at the final "handing over of the keys" ceremony. (The event took place two days before I married Wilfred Thomas.) The ceremony's venue was in front of the former USIA headquarters, which is now State Building #44 at 301 C Street SW. The entire city block in front of the building was closed to traffic. It was filled with USIA colleagues. We made our remarks, we placed the State Department emblem on the building, and the real work of integration began.

In the last fifteen years, nine political appointees have been the undersecretary of public diplomacy and public affairs. No undersecretary has stayed at the job longer than two years, and many stayed for only one. The undersecretary has almost no authority to do anything, making it difficult to make public diplomacy a vital aspect of foreign policy. Public diplomacy happens in the field under the authority of ambassadors who pay attention to the undersecretary or not, as they choose.

The undersecretaries have been respected journalists, former White House press secretaries, and media moguls, and some have been advertising and marketing gurus. However, even the best communication expert could not present America and its foreign policy goals as marketable products. Much of the world believes our interests abroad are motivated by a need for oil, other natural resources, and political and economic stability in a region.

To change human behavior and opinions requires patience and genuine dialogue. Flashy marketing approaches do not work. Correcting misperceptions about America requires cultural sensitivity, patience, relationship building, and trust. Contrary to popular belief, America's advanced technology, celebrated universities, military might, and economic stability do not win the hearts and minds of others. I quickly learned that most world cultures value their long histories. They respect the lessons of their past. They rely on historical precedent in making decisions. Citizens of Asia, Africa, Latin America, and Western Europe often remind us of how young we are as a nation. Americans have a great deal to learn from other countries. We work best when we work in partnership.

9

Off to Dakar

I believe in American exceptionalism with every fiber of my being. But what makes us exceptional is not our ability to flout international norms and the rule of law; it's our willingness to affirm them through our actions.—PRESIDENT BARACK OBAMA at West Point, May 28, 2014

In April 1998 President Clinton made a state visit to Senegal, underscoring it as one of our closest allies among the Francophone nations of Africa. Speaking at Gorée Island, a former slave port off the coast of Dakar, the president recognized the struggles of African Americans for equality and pledged his support of efforts by Africans toward peace and democracy. On July 1, 1999, he sent my name to the Senate as his nominee to be U.S. ambassador to the Republic of Senegal.

At my confirmation hearing on August 5, I told the Senate Committee on Foreign Relations that I found the current Foreign Service quite different from the service that existed when I entered in 1963. The number of minorities and women in positions of authority had been abysmally low. I found myself being spokesperson for a nation that had not yet come to terms with its own richness, its extraordinary cultural diversity, or its own complexity.

"Thankfully, my years in the service of my country have coincided with fundamental changes at home," I told the Senate committee. "The Civil Rights movement and the women's movement permanently altered the way Americans see and define themselves. These movements also changed how people around the world see and define us. The vital work performed by Foreign Service officers overseas, often under difficult and dangerous conditions, is enriched by the extent that they represent the diversity of this nation."

Soon afterward I headed to Dakar with my new husband. The closing months of 1999 had brought three life-changing experiences: marriage, a move to West Africa, and finally, running an embassy.

I married Wilfred J. Thomas on October 3, 1999, two months before my only living brother, retired Massachusetts Superior Court judge Harry J. Elam, swore me in as U.S. ambassador to Senegal. My brother, who had witnessed my confirmation hearing with Wilfred, gave me away at the wedding ceremony. Two ministers conducted our wedding, the late Reverend A. Knighton Stanley of Peoples Congregational Church in Washington DC and the late Reverend Dr. John Gravely, founder of Living Light Ministries and former interim pastor at Northeastern Presbyterian Church, Sargent Memorial Presbyterian Church, and Church of the Redeemer Presbyterian. John Gravely was another of my closest friends and confidants. Like Ofield Dukes, John Gravely constantly reminded me never to let others define me. He was among those who guided me through many personal and professional challenges. From my disappointment over the slow pace of my promotions as well as a broken engagement in 1979, John kept me centered and encouraged me to soldier on. Though very much my contemporary, he was like a brother. His tragic death, along with his wife, Blondeen, in a May 2012 car accident shocked Wilfred and me to our cores.

This was my very first marriage, at the "young" age of fifty-eight. Our two hundred guests attended the wedding and dinner held at the Park Hyatt on Twenty-First Street NW near Georgetown in Washington DC. The groom was sixty-five and the father of four adult children. Born in Trinidad, Wilfred, formerly in banking, computing, and travel businesses in the Caribbean, had been a U.S. citizen for nearly twenty-five years. I am convinced that it was truly divine intervention that brought Wilfred into my life. For nearly two decades, until I met Wilfred, I had absolutely no interest in getting married. My career kept me more than occupied. It seemed all of the other gents I dated had hidden agendas. I realized they were interested in how I could enhance their career goals through my contacts with individuals in the White House or in the U.S. diplomatic community. When we met, Wilfred knew nothing of my professional career. He was curious about me as a person. That was a good thing. He reminded me of my big brother Harry, and that was a very good thing. He had the discipline and strength to deliver messages to me that gave me reason to rethink my approach to some issues. You will notice I said "some" issues, not all. As I am reminded every day, we are works in progress. That is also a good thing.

Wilfred and I met in New York City on New Year's Eve 1997. On my trip back to the States from Brussels for my assignment to USIA, I planned to visit with my sister in a Denver nursing home. A friend I had met at the International Protestant Church of Brussels, Tina Walls, then manager for Philip Morris Europe, knew that spending time with my sister would be a sobering experience. Tina suggested I first take a break and spend some time with her in New York for the New Year's weekend. I thought about declining. Floating around New York City on New Year's Eve with another single woman was not something that Harriet Elam would do. Tina would not have it. And as it turned out, sitting at a corporate table as Tina's guest would change my life.

Among the interesting conversationalists at the table was one Wilfred James Thomas, who knew a lot about international affairs. He mentioned he had a daughter who was a cardiologist and a member of Delta Sigma Theta (my sorority and the sorority of the first African American woman attorney general, Loretta Lynch). I suggested she should meet one of my colleagues, the director of women's health at the National Institutes of Health, Dr. Vivian W. Pinn. He wrote his daughter's name on the back of one of his business cards, which I kept.

We danced a couple of times. He was a good dancer as well as an excellent conversationalist. These were very good things. He has teased me since that night of December 31, 1997, regarding my ability to talk. Not a lot of men I had met could carry on a conversation with me about India, Pakistan, and other crisis countries around the world, but this chap did. That piqued my interest.

Later I was host for an event for a colleague back from Madrid who was going to be my deputy in the counselor's office. I needed to have several men at this event, so I called and invited Wilfred. (He was scheduled to be in Washington to see a doctor at Providence Hospital regarding a problem with his knee.) Also at the event was my nephew Jay, Dr. Harry J. Elam. Wilfred first spent a lot of time on the balcony talking with my dear friend from Athens Margaret Murphy. Later I learned he had also engaged in a curious conversation with my nephew. I was intrigued. I was curious. At the end of the evening, I invited him to come back for coffee the following morning before his return trip to New York City. He accepted that invitation, and we had a three-hour conversation on the balcony of my Crystal City apartment in northern Virginia. I heard his life's story. He was from a part of the world that was very much a part of my brother's world, which was another good thing. Wilfred was from Trinidad, as was my brother's late mother-in-law. The more we spoke, the more we seemed to have many connections. After my long hiatus from any romantic connection, I will admit my mind on that score began to change.

In the days that followed, we spoke frequently by phone. My housekeeper noticed our long phone conversations. Obviously, I must have been interested to be chatting away on the phone.

A few months later, I attended my thirty-fifth college reunion, staying with my classmates in the college dorms. During late-night talks, I told them about Wilfred. Shortly after my arrival at the reunion, I learned that my oldest brother, Charles Elam, had passed away. My classmates encouraged me to call Wilfred and tell him about my brother's death. Wilfred had said, "Should you ever need a shoulder to lean on, don't hesitate to call me." The Simmons classmates had never met him, but these women encouraged my interest in this gentleman. There I was, calling from a telephone booth in the Simmons College dormitory (there were no cell phones then). I was fifty-six years old and acting like a freshman. When I told him of Charles's passing, he expressed his sympathy. My brother Harry insisted that I attend the reunion and made sure funeral arrangements allowed me time to get to Atlanta for the service.

When Wilfred and I became engaged, these women hosted a shower for me at the Regency Hyatt in Pentagon City and invited Wilfred. They smoked him out, just as my nephew had done. Clearly, he passed their tests.

Before the engagement, however, I knew it would be wise for Wilfred to meet Harry. In September 1998 Harry and Barbara came to Washington DC for the swearing in of Boston's Charles Stith to become ambassador to Tanzania. (Ambassador Stith in 2015 was one of four editors of *African Americans in U.S. Foreign Policy: From the Era of Frederick Douglass to the Age of Obama*.) Introducing Harry to Wilfred let everyone know I was interested in him and that this relationship was serious. Wilfred later told me he thought he had already met my brother at a party I gave at which he asked Wilfred a lot of probing questions. He now realized he had met my nephew. Jay and his father are almost twins. Both were playing the big brother role, checking Wilfred out for the family.

I will be the first to admit that being married to me is nothing like Hollywood's storybook image of "and they lived happily ever after." Wilfred would be the first to agree that it is hard work. I had been single for the thirty-seven years of my working life, a life that included managing a U.S. government agency, being independent, and running around the world. I have never been a global celebrity with a huge persona, but I am not a wallflower, either.

Few of the gents I knew earlier in my career would have been able to handle this independent, self-confident professional in international affairs. One of my friends calls him "first husband" and a niece calls him "Sir Wilfred." Even before he received those absolutely appropriate sobriquets, he acknowledged that he is a significantly proud man. He has preserved his independent pride and presence despite the inherent challenges of being married to an equally proud woman.

Trust me when I say there is nothing that intimidates my equal half (our name for each other). One morning, only months after settling into the ambassador's residence in Dakar, Wilfred and I woke up to see intruders scaling the six-foot wall. Wilfred, a former Trinidad police officer and a top marksman, jumped out of bed to investigate while I scrambled to get into the secure room. Wilfred soon determined that the intruders were striking guards scaling the fence to punish our guards for having stayed on duty during a guard strike. All the guards at the residences were host country citizens, security forces from a Senegalese company. Marine guards do not guard the ambassador's residence. By the time Wilfred came back inside, our diplomatic security had come out to the residence. They made sure our guards were not harmed, but the incident was a bit frightening. Almost all ambassadors have a "brush with death" story, some far more alarming than this one. Let me repeat, nothing intimidates Wilfred Thomas.

Our flourishing courtship took place while I was deeply involved in the consolidation of USIA with the Department of State. I traveled abroad frequently to PAO conferences. While in Madrid and exchanging greetings with the director of the Prado Museum, I received a page call. Wilfred had tracked me down in Madrid. This man was romantic, resourceful, and determined to find out more about me. He found out, I suspect from my college friends, that I liked to entertain. Some of my FSO colleagues say I would set the table a week in advance and put a sheet over the table to keep the dust off. I'm not that bad, but when I had to do it, mainly when I was alone and did not have Wilfred to be the chef par excellence, I had to get things in place well in advance. I can tell you that, these days, it is comforting to have a spouse who calls my office at the close of the day to be sure the evening menu fits my desires. Given the demanding lives of diplomats representing the United States abroad and at home, I am most fortunate to have an accommodating mate.

Our first journey together took us to Grenada, where Wilfred had lived from age nine to twenty. He knew our relationship was getting serious, and he wanted me to experience his roots. The natural vistas were stunning, but the sand flies took their toll on me. Wilfred joked that they knew this was new territory for me, and the sand fly bites were their way of welcoming me to Grenada. I could have done well without that part of the welcome, but that did not take away from the beauty of the Spice Island.

Wilfred has a wealth of British jokes that he learned as a child in Grenada and Trinidad, and I was attracted to his sense of humor. We developed our private code words, just as the Secret Service creates code names for the president, vice president, first lady, and other high-level officials. If one of us uttered one of those words, only the other knew its meaning.

The *Washington Post* reported my busy schedule: on October 1, 1999, I turned over the keys to the USIA building to Secretary Albright in front of eight hundred USIA employees, who filled the city block outside the building. Two days later, on October 3, I got married, and then I began final preparations to jet off to become the ambassador to Senegal.

Just before the official ceremony in front of USIA headquarters, I shared a candid moment with Secretary Albright. I told her I had second thoughts concerning an interview I had given to a *Washington Post* reporter. Albright reminded me of her own life. The press, she told me, had reported her "public bleeding all over Washington" when she and her former husband, Joe Albright, divorced. She said I should not be concerned. Certainly, she had been hurt and embarrassed by the press attention to her private life, but it showed she was human. That was the confidence boost I needed as I headed to center stage for the USIA closing ceremony. It was a woman-to-woman connection that endeared me to this great woman. She cared about other women in the diplomatic service. Wilfred still calls me when "my favorite boss" is slated to be interviewed on television.

Shortly after our splendid honeymoon at the Four Seasons in St. Kitts and Nevis, we prepared for the December 3, 1999, swearing-in ceremony. It was a challenge to keep the number of guests to four hundred, given the space limitations of the State Department's Benjamin Franklin Room. Once that ceremony ended, a smaller group of out-of-town guests and very close friends joined us for a luncheon and the announcement of the Harriet Elam-Thomas Study Abroad Fund at Simmons College in Boston.

My classmate Gerry Morenski's daughter, Kathleen Morenski, today a twenty-one-year career Foreign Service officer veteran, was a junior officer at that time. She was the one who solicited the significant funds needed to establish the scholarship fund. Unbeknownst to me, Kathleen had sent out a simulated "secret" telegram to my friends and colleagues requesting contributions. I was touched and moved to tears when Kathleen and her mother made that surprise announcement at the luncheon. That scholarship fund continues to this day, and through it Simmons students have been able to study abroad over the past fifteen years.

Our next journey would take us to West Africa. We left Washington on January 3, 2000, for Dakar, via Paris and Stuttgart. One of my colleagues, Bisa Williams, a bright young FSO assigned to Paris, hosted a delightful reception in Paris. (Bisa later became ambassador to Niger and deputy assistant secretary for Africa.) From Paris, we were off to Stuttgart for the traditional chief of mission briefing, done at the European Command headquarters. At that time the African Command did not exist, and the responsibility for Africa was shared by the other combatant commands. We stayed with the deputy commander, Navy admiral Charles Abbott, now retired. As we entered his residence, we thought we were entering a German castle. We were escorted to the vast, elegantly decorated guest wing. Wilfred and I remained appropriately composed despite how amazed we were at this setting. The dinner guests included senior military and a few diplomats, all well informed about Senegal.

The following day I went to the briefing, and Wilfred was able to join me. As we walked into the briefing room, the setting was somewhat intimidating. A room was filled with officers in uniform seated at desks in a large semicircle, each desk equipped with sophisticated monitors. A jumbo screen filled the front of the room. I steadied myself by remembering how I got through the Senate confirmation hearings.

Right after the briefing, Wilfred told me he was proud of me because of the questions I posed. I owe thanks to the desk officer for Senegal, John Jones (later U.S. ambassador to Guyana), and the deputy chief of mission, Terrence McCulley (subsequently ambassador to Togo, Nigeria, and the Ivory Coast). They provided me with detailed reports before I reached Stuttgart. Their excellent work earlier in their careers proved they were capable of managing embassies in the future. I was very fortunate to have them as my resource. As a woman FSO, I knew I had to be prepared. I probably overprepared. There was always that glass ceiling, no matter how many million cracks currently exist. On that day, the ceiling felt mighty close.

The briefing officers covered the potential terrorist threats in Africa at that time. They analyzed the August 7, 1998, truck bombings at U.S. embassies in Tanzania and Kenya, which took the lives of many American diplomats as well as Tanzanian and Kenyan nationals and employees. These attacks were linked to al-Qaeda. I had known managing an embassy would be a major task, but I left that briefing sobered by the heavy responsibility before me.

Strengthening U.S.-Senegalese relations was important, but the security of every embassy staffer was of equal importance. The excitement of the wedding, swearing-in ceremony, and farewell events faded into the background. I was just a day or two from taking on the direction of an embassy. I could not rest on my previous reputation. I was no longer young, I was certainly still a black woman, and once again, I faced a brand-new mission. I was determined to succeed.

From Stuttgart, we returned to Paris to catch our flight to Dakar. At Charles de Gaulle Airport, before we boarded our flight, I saw a familiar face. Could this be Samba Ba, the late president Léopold Sédar Senghor's chief of protocol? I had not seen Samba Ba in twenty-eight years. I approached him and learned it was indeed Monsieur Ba. He was no longer the dashing and debonair young officer attired in his white military uniform, but he had aged with dignity. During my time as assistant cultural attaché in the midseventies, Samba Ba was one of my key contacts. Unlike other Senegalese, Ba never asked for special visa favors. I appreciated his discretion, and I was pleased to see him again.

On board, per U.S. government regulations, we were in business class. Samba Ba was in first class. Wilfred and I were about to experience *teranga*, Senegalese society's "hospitality," in which guests are treated with respect and honor. Apparently, Samba passed a message that the new U.S. ambassador to Senegal was on board and that

Wilfred and I should disembark before the first-class passengers. As we entered the VIP lounge, the usual welcoming party had gathered, along with journalists and electronic media representatives. Monsieur Ba took the microphone and spoke about my time in Dakar as a junior officer. He actually upstaged the designated welcoming party from the Ministry of Foreign Affairs, including Cheikh Tidiane Gadio, who later became the foreign minister. What a wonderful welcome back to Senegal!

I found the Senegal of 2000 a very different country from the one I knew from 1975 to 1977. Many former embassy contacts had passed away, but some were now in important government positions. In Senegal, people in positions of authority looked like me, except they were men. However, I was not the first African American or woman to serve as ambassador to Senegal. Others include Mercer Cook (1964–66), O. Rudolph Aggrey (1973–77), Walter Carrington (1980), George Moose (1988–91), Katherine Shirley (1991), Janice Jacobs (2006), and later Marcia Bernicat (2008–11).

In the late 1970s I owned a condominium in the same Park Sutton residences in Silver Spring, Maryland, where Ambassador Mercer Cook lived. I was pleased whenever I saw this scholarly and elegant gentleman of the old school in the lobby or elevator of our building. Ambassador O. Rudolph Aggrey was equally inspiring. Both men navigated the treacherous minefield of overt and subtle discrimination that existed throughout all U.S. government agencies in the early 1950s. Aggrey had passed the rigorous Foreign Service exam, but initially he was not hired. It could have been a bitter start to what would be a long and distinguished career. In his oral history at the end of his career, he dismissed the episode of discrimination as "indicative of the times and of some of the vicissitudes that our country has come through." He added, "I was told, at that time, that, although I'd passed the examination, that I was not going to be hired in the domestic branch of the Department of State. And some friends got wind of this development and contacted officials in the Department of State, who decided to look into it. The end of that effort was that it came to the attention of the Secretary of State, who was then Dean

Acheson, through his special assistant, who was Lucius Battle. And the word came down, from the secretary through Lucius Battle, that the man is qualified, he should be hired."

He was soon recruited for overseas service specifically because "I had some African background on my father's side." His father was J. E. Kwegyir Aggrey. He came to America from Ghana in the early 1900s to study, staying long enough to marry a Virginia teacher and become a professor at Livingstone College in North Carolina. He founded a college in Ghana. One of his four children was this future ambassador, who grew up in an international household because during the segregation era his parents opened their home to visiting Africans and other people of color from other parts of the world. As it turned out, what was first judged to be a disqualifying factor qualified him for a career as a diplomat of great service to the U.S. government and people.

Another of my inspiring role models was Terence Alphonso Todman, who rose to the rank of career ambassador, serving the United States as ambassador to Chad, Guinea, Costa Rica, Spain, Denmark, and Argentina as well as assistant secretary of state for inter-American affairs during the Carter administration. I was honored to substitute for Ambassador Ruth A. Davis and to speak at Ambassador Todman's eighty-fifth birthday celebration in St. Thomas and to sit next to him at the Black Ambassadors' Association luncheon at the Cosmos Club on May 5, 2014. Blessed to be one of Ambassador Todman's mentees, I was again honored to accompany a small delegation from Washington and to speak briefly at his funeral in St. Thomas in August 2014. How well I remember in the 1970s getting permission to take an extra hour for lunch in order to hear Ambassador Todman speak to young diplomats of color at a Thursday Luncheon Group gathering in the State Department. The lessons he shared with us in that meeting guided me throughout the rest of my diplomatic career.

In his oral history, Ambassador Todman noted that when he started in the State Department in the 1950s, "the only thing they had blacks doing . . . was serving as messengers and secretaries." The entrenched biases of those times prohibited him from eating lunch with white colleagues. Even later, despite building his expertise in Arabic and Arab affairs, he was relegated to African posts.

Senegal, a country that respects its history and tradition, has its own biases, including its male-dominated politics. Of the sixty members of the diplomatic corps accredited to Senegal during my time as ambassador, six of us were women. We knew we must respect traditions and, as women, we had to be particularly careful not to "step out of the bounds," despite being the representatives of our countries. It was a delicate duty, which we carried out effectively.

Yet I would see one tradition fall.

Wilfred and I arrived in Senegal just as the Protocol Office had changed the rules regarding presentation of credentials at the palace. The beachfront Palais Présidentiel rests within the arch of the Italy-shaped boot heel at the eastern edge of Dakar. The metropolitan center's harbor, among the largest seaports and industrial centers of West Africa, is to the northeast. Wilfred became the first spouse allowed to accompany a new ambassador during the credentials presentation. What a relief. This was an important event in my life, and I wanted my spouse to be present. The ceremony included an inspection of the honor guard. For Wilfred, it was nostalgic, reminding him of his times as a young police officer in Trinidad when he participated in similar state ceremonies as an honor guard on parade.

The embassy in Dakar had 534 employees, the standard number for a midsized post. USAID had the largest component: 223 staffers. One of the ambassador's first tasks, even before presenting his or her credentials to the head of state, is to chair a country team meeting. Country teams are composed of the heads of embassy sections. The atmosphere of my first meeting with the country team was polite but very cool. The section and agency heads stood respectfully, as is the practice. I realized that as a woman, I had to work doubly hard to gain their trust and respect. I outlined the ground rules. This embassy should not have lapses in security or administrative requirements. Special attention must be given to all written communications to Washington. My name appeared at the bottom of every official message. The grammar, spelling, and punctuation had to be correct. Washington recipients would not consider the fact (as we did when I was a desk officer) that the message might have been written by a Foreign Service national (locally engaged staffer). English is not their first language. I also reminded them of the strict guidelines for the use of official vehicles. I instructed the IT staffer to install a separate phone line for my personal Internet access. As a woman ambassador and as a person of color, I would be held to a higher standard. Any infractions under my watch would be subject to detailed scrutiny. As of January 2000, I had received no security violations during my thirty-seven years of service. (To my dismay, I did get one just before I departed Senegal. By error, I did not secure one classified document. Even though it was on the secure floor of the embassy, it still constituted a violation.) I was painfully aware that everything every ambassador did while abroad reflected on the United States. Every action taken would impact one's reputation. Sadly, during my time as counselor of USIA, I witnessed too many examples of poor judgment thwarting otherwise promising careers.

The foreign national staff in the embassy was predominantly Senegalese, but there were others from Guinea-Bissau, the nation on Senegal's southern border. (The U.S. embassy in Dakar also handles diplomatic relations with the Republic of Guinea-Bissau.) Senegal is a predominantly Muslim nation, but the locally engaged staff includes some from other non-Muslim majority countries. The embassy recognized Christian and Muslim holidays, reflecting Senegal's tolerance of religious minorities. Interfaith and interracial marriage is widely accepted. Christians attend Muslim feasts and Muslims join Christian celebrations. Some Muslim children attend Catholic schools, adding to the cultural exchange. With the exception of the Casamance Region, religious conflict was minimal. A separatist independence movement in the Casamance Region south of the Gambia River has flared up with sporadic violence since the 1980s. The government has devoted a great deal of time and energy to bring peace to the region, holding talks in the region and sending ministerial representatives to talks in Banjul, Gambia.

Senegal is not as well known as Rwanda, Sierra Leone, Liberia, Guinea, and the many other conflict regions of Africa precisely because there has not been a major religious or ethnic conflict or an Ebola outbreak. The separatist insurgency in the southern part of the country continues to be a security concern, and despite Senegal's long tradition of being both stable and democratic, it is not without its problems. The persecution of journalists, the suppression of the political opposition, and government corruption continue to undermine Senegal's reputation.

During my time in Dakar, the U.S. embassy, one of more than sixty diplomatic missions that give the city of some 1.5 million people an international feel, was in the center of the city, which tops a plateau overlooking the Atlantic. My residence was in the beachside Fann district, one of a handful of tree-lined neighborhoods scattered among tall, modern commercial and government buildings. A new embassy compound, which includes the ambassador's residence, opened in 2013 on a ten-acre site near Pointe des Almadies, Africa's westernmost point at the northwestern end of the Cap Vert peninsula. Both physically and symbolically, the new embassy is a gateway to the West.

Dakar is a mosaic of old and new Africa: a mixture of Islamic influence dating to the eleventh century, a period of French colonial rule from the nineteenth century until 1960, followed by a more modern, worldly African society. The Senegalese have a growing connection to America, but they remain closely tied to France, and the city is the cultural capital of French-speaking West Africa. French is the official language, but the most common language is the native Wolof. Dakar has its own urban dialect of Wolof mixed with French and Arabic.

Invariably, whenever I had an appointment with President Abdoulaye Wade, I encountered French ambassador Jean de Gliniasty, who from 2009 to 2013 was the French ambassador to Russia. These not-so-coincidental meetings reminded me to deliver my messages with great caution. Whatever I said to the president might well be shared with the French ambassador. We could not afford to forget that the French had a long colonial relationship with Senegal. Two of Senegal's presidents married French women. U.S. and French diplomats have good social interaction and shared interests, but despite

Senegal's independence, the French wished to limit U.S. influence on the nation. France wanted to remain Senegal's first ally, and I understood that.

Ambassador de Gliniasty and I made a tacit joint pact to be mutually supportive in our relations with our Senegalese hosts. In fact, I recall working with de Gliniasty and our respective delegation members during late-night negotiations over the 2001 contested presidential elections in Madagascar. It was not unusual for Dakar to be selected as the site of international conferences and negotiations because it had modern conference centers equipped with simultaneous translation facilities and contemporary hotels. In 2001 the first-ever Senate elections in Madagascar, part of a policy to extend democratic governance, finally took place after a long delay. In the December 2001 presidential election, opposition candidate Marc Ravalomanana claimed that he had been denied an outright victory by polling irregularities. He declared himself president in February 2002 after refusing to take part in a postponed second-round runoff vote.

Dakar was a challenge, not only for me but for Wilfred. While I settled in at the embassy, Wilfred managed what then was called the American Club or just the Club, which was about five miles from the embassy. Now called the Club Atlantique, it is run by the embassy's employee association for U.S. personnel, missionaries, students, and private sector Americans and foreign nationals living in Dakar. It is an oasis for the people at the embassies, for the expats, for the corporate folk, and for the international community to unwind, play tennis and table tennis, swim and play basketball and other sports, or enjoy picnics and beach parties. It is right next door to the International School of Dakar, a private school. Roughly a third of the students are American dependents, and the rest are of dozens of other nationalities. From time to time, the children came to have lunch at the American Club's snack bar, which was a treat for them. Of course, Wilfred was the disciplinarian, along with the teachers.

Fourth of July celebrations for the nondiplomatic U.S. community were traditionally held at the American Club. The event held at the ambassador's residence was for Senegalese dignitaries, international diplomats, journalists, and academic leaders. It was formal. The atmosphere at the American Club was relaxed, and no one needed to worry about getting barbeque sauce, mustard, and ketchup on their grand *boubous* (traditional, elegant robes) or cocktail attire one would wear to the embassy residence.

The club's location on the Atlantic offered an attractive outdoor setting when we arrived, but Wilfred built up the reputation of the clubhouse. He raised the professionalism of the club's management and staff. It became a vibrant institution. Wilfred had been in the travel and tourism industry. He had owned a travel agency. He had been president of the Caribbean Tourism Organization for greater New York and part of New England and Connecticut. He had worked with travel and tourism representatives for Dutch, English, French, and Spanish businesses in the Caribbean. He was in somewhat the role of a private sector tourism ambassador.

Eighteen months after my arrival, the first deputy chief of mission, Terence "Terry" McCulley, took on his next assignment. I had been fortunate to have Terry in Dakar. Terry is one of the gems of the Foreign Service. He is committed to serving his country by representing the United States in challenging posts without expecting anything in return. Materials he provided prior to my confirmation hearing helped me respond to the probing questions the senators posed during those tense few hours of my life.

My political officer in Dakar, Deborah Malac became the U.S. ambassador to Liberia and later Uganda (2015). Debbie comported herself with the utmost sensitivity and dignity during the Ebola crisis. I am extremely pleased to have had the opportunity to work with Terry and Debbie, for they epitomize what one expects of a U.S. diplomat.

There are only two embassy positions that an ambassador can choose, the deputy chief of mission and the office management specialist (read: executive assistant). Ruth Walker was my office management specialist. Whenever the Foreign Service Institute or the private sector wishes to train individuals to carry out this critical position, Ruth Walker would be my nominee as the perfect role model. She remains in constant demand at the highest levels in the Department of State, despite her retirement in December 2005. Few office managers would volunteer to go to an embassy two or three weeks in advance of the ambassador to facilitate her arrival, as she did for me. Few office management specialists have the wealth of Foreign Service experience needed to be able to prioritize the scores of appointment requests along with the almost endless list of official calls required when a new ambassador arrives at post. None of the executive assistants I have known could match her skills as the Praetorian Guard in the front office, managing my schedule without alienating government ministers, military officers, senior business leaders, staffers, and others who say they absolutely must see the ambassador. Ruth's communication skills and presence allowed her to carry out that role with aplomb. Very few felt the pulse on the indigenous culture the way she did. She made recommendations to recognize Senegalese whose work might have gone unnoticed. Ruth Walker deserves much of the credit for my success as chief of mission in Dakar. Without reservation, Ruth Walker is at the top of her profession, and few others in my forty-two-year diplomatic career matched her intellect, discretion, poise, and sensitivity. She is a class act in every sense of that phrase.

The second deputy chief of mission, Alan Lattimer, later served in Haiti and Iraq and is now a foreign policy advisor at U.S. Army Africa Command. I was particularly careful in selecting Alan as Terry's successor. After I reviewed a host of evaluations on Alan, including one written by the highly respected Ambassador Princeton Lyman, I believed I made a wise choice. Alan's performance in Dakar followed the pattern chronicled in Lyman's report. Suddenly, however, the management counselor and general services officer resisted Alan's new regulations for property acquisition and warehouse inventory control. Once again, I called on my Fletcher training in conflict resolution to resolve what could have been a major internal crisis.

During one of Terry's absences and prior to Alan's arrival, Chris Datta served as my deputy chief of mission. Chris was so effective and sensitive in that position that I later told him I wished I had known of his interest in being deputy chief of mission before I traveled to Washington to review files and select Terry's successor. Chris continued with a stellar career, serving in highly challenging posts in Africa. He is a soft-spoken public diplomacy USIA officer, like me, but also a man of strength willing to accept challenges. He was chargé at our embassy in Monrovia, Liberia, during the horrendous rule of Charles Taylor and that nation's civil war. The duty would fall to him in 2003 to tell the president of Liberia, a war criminal, that he would have to step down and leave the country.

Chris also served as chargé at our new embassy in Juba, Sudan. Like Terry, Chris is a white American with a genuine commitment to the development of the people on the African continent. There are many diplomats like them, but their stories are seldom told in U.S. newspapers. Chris and his wife at the time adopted a young man from Sierra Leone who had suffered serious leg injuries during the war in Sierra Leone. I was delighted to see the adopted son, Abu, at Chris's wedding to his new bride on May 23, 2015.

Chris has authored a book based on the life of a young woman during the U.S. Civil War, and he is working on a memoir that covers his time in highly troubled regions, including India, Jordan, Lebanon, Eritrea, Sudan, South Sudan, Rwanda, Sierra Leone, and Liberia.

Don Clark, USAID director, projected one of the most positive images of Americans working abroad. Respected by the indigenous population and all of the Senegalese ministers, Don led a terrific operation. No doubt his marriage to Connie Clark, the daughter of a former diplomat from Burkina Faso, added to Don's credibility among the Senegalese. Connie's sincere outreach throughout the embassy and the Senegalese community assured USAID's dynamic work environment.

Fortunately, I have been blessed to have had the best and brightest USIA officers work with me throughout my career. Michael Pelletier, Chris Datta's successor, also rises to the top on my list in terms of professionalism, commitment, and sensitivity. The lives of these men who served me with such loyalty and dignity would merit their own book. Because of them, I was able to leave what I have been told was a lasting impact of U.S.-Senegalese relations upon my departure in December 2002.

Michael, a natural linguist, is fluent in Arabic and French. I was thrilled to be in the State Department a few years ago just in time to attend a ceremony where Michael received the linguist of the year award. He is fluent not only in Arabic but in various dialects of Arabic.

It was Michael's idea that I give an address on the second anniversary of the September 11 tragedy at the Islamic Center in Dakar. I gave the speech in French, but Michael introduced me in Arabic and made certain that all of my remarks would be simultaneously translated into Arabic as well as Wolof, the main indigenous language of Senegal. The speech on tolerance could not have been better timed, but the fact that it was available to the largest audience imaginable in Dakar, thanks to Michael's foresight in having it translated into Arabic and Wolof, was unprecedented. Michael is now (2017) our deputy chief of mission in New Delhi, India, where he resides with his wife, Suja, and two sons. They were wonderful hosts when I visited Dubai for the World Education Forum in 2009.

Military men headed the Office of Security Assistance. The defense attaché was Todd Coker, an African American Marine lieutenant colonel and graduate of the Naval Academy. He is now retired from active duty. In mid-2014 he became principal director at the Office of the Deputy Assistant Secretary of Defense for African Affairs. Members of the country team also included the Federal Aviation Agency's regional representative, USAID's inspector general director, Treasury Department representatives, and the Peace Corps director.

Not everyone met my standards. In a one-on-one meeting with me, a young officer of color asked if he could have a firearm. I immediately asked, "Why are you in this office?" His response: "Well, because, you know, I thought if I asked you . . ." I stopped him in midsentence and said, "The DCM's office is directly across the hall." (The DCM is the deputy chief of mission, the second in command of a U.S. embassy.) I rejected his request. But I asked him why in the name of heaven he did not go through channels. Well, this young man already had made the request through channels and had received a negative response. He thought by coming directly to me, he might get a positive response. Oh, how wrong!

That was not his only misstep. Near the end of his tour, he announced he had lost keys to the embassy warehouse. I barely maintained my composure. Immediately I told him to alert the regional security officer. He got absolutely no sympathy from me. I am sure he thought I was the worst person on the planet. I am proud to say he is now doing very well in the Foreign Service and is a midlevel officer who served one tour as an instructor at the Foreign Service Institute. The admonitions he received and the example I portrayed seem to have moved his career on to a positive track.

As the president's representative to the government of Senegal, I used the same approach of being totally honest in my evaluations of Senegal's progress toward sustainable development and economic stability. On the surface, the Senegalese accepted my candid assessments of their lack of tangible evidence of improvement in their educational, health, and economic programs. I reminded Senegalese ministers of the inadequacies of the Senegalese government's budget allocations and follow-up on health care delivery and education. That was the primary reason why Senegal did not qualify for debt relief under the World Bank's standards for a Heavily Indebted Poor Country (HIPC). The World Bank and the International Monetary Fund established those rules in 1996. Once a country met those requirements, it became eligible for debt relief. The World Bank representative, with counsel from the embassy's economic and political sections, determined that Senegal did not qualify for relief. During my mid-2000 consultation with National Security Advisor Dr. Jendayi Frazier, who later became ambassador to South Africa and assistant secretary for African affairs, I told her about the World Bank report. With Senegal's peaceful transition of power when President Abdoulaye Wade was elected in 2000 and given election fraud in other sub-Saharan nations, National Security Council (NSC) staff considered Senegal a success. In reality, the political story was the only success. I listened respectfully as Jendayi Frazier suggested that I be more understanding of Senegal, especially in light of the other failed democracies on the continent.

In 2013 Senegal contained the potential outbreak of Ebola when it quickly found an infected Guinean who had crossed the border into Senegal, isolated him, and set up effective controls against other potential cases. However, during my three years in Senegal, the nation had shown minimal improvement in its educational and health care delivery systems.

I also had to school one of Wade's senior officials on protocol. Soon after Wade's election in early 2000, I was reading a Senegalese newspaper and I saw that Cheikh Tidiane Gadio had been named the new foreign minister of Senegal. What a pleasant surprise and shock. This was the gent who was upstaged when I arrived at the airport. And I had ignored his efforts to contact me before my arrival. Now he was to be my main contact with the Senegalese government. A Fulbright scholar at the University of Ohio, Gadio had tried to contact me when he learned I had been nominated to become ambassador. Following the strict guidance for all nominees, I never responded to his emails or phone messages. Later Gadio and I met at a presentation I did in Atlanta for the International Public Policy Institute, which gave me the opportunity to politely tell him I could not be in contact with him for official reasons.

I chuckled to myself as I prepared for my first official meeting with the new foreign minister. The two of us worked extremely well together until I learned that President Wade was en route to the United States for a meeting with high-level U.S. government officials at the National Security Council and perhaps at the White House.

Strict protocol rules require the foreign minister to inform the U.S. ambassador in advance of a head of state's visit to the United States. Gadio did not, and when he realized his error, he called me to apologize immediately after his arrival in the United States. I was not my most diplomatic self in that conversation. I let Gadio know that briefings for these U.S. officials must be done by the embassy prior to any meetings with heads of state. How in the world could the political and economic officers and other key Dakar embassy staff get such briefings to the NSC and the White House if we had no advance notice of the visit? Personal relationships sometimes trump official protocol in traditional cultures. Wade knew several of the officials he planned to meet and probably did not even consider it a serious diplomatic slight in having Gadio schedule the NSC and other Cabinet-level meetings. I seriously doubted this was an intentional slight, but I let Gadio know this should never happen again. He apologized, and it never happened again.

Gadio was foreign minister from 2000 to 2009. He was asked to leave the government, allegedly because he had a disagreement with President Wade's son, Karim, who had been in jail for eighteen months awaiting trial on corruption. Gadio broke with President Wade's party and established a new party. In 2012 Gadio was an unsuccessful candidate for Senegal's presidency and lost to Macky Sall. Gadio remains actively involved in international affairs.

After I accompanied many high-level U.S. government officials to palace meetings with President Wade, I began to question why he routinely showed a mock-up of the "centers of learning" to be established in villages throughout Senegal. The mock-up looked impressive, but in the three years I served as ambassador, I never saw one of the learning centers actually built, and I frequently traveled the interior of Senegal. Despite Jendayi Frazier's perspective, I considered it my duty to recommend that the NSC not support loans and debt relief that Senegal could receive from the World Bank. Little did I know the President Wade was a personal friend of the World Bank president, James Wolfensohn. One personal phone call from President Wade to Wolfensohn sealed the deal. Wade announced that Senegal would receive $40 million. Despite the hard work and research done by the World Bank representative and embassy colleagues, we did not influence the final decision. Lesson learned: personal relationships can trump the best empirical data.

President Wade was the president, and I had to maintain open and respectful dialogue with him. I did so, with my usual candor. I once goaded him to take action. I told this African head of state about fifteen years my senior, "Mr. President, you don't want the Europeans to think you can't run your country." I cautioned President Wade that outside observers would become suspicious of his rhetoric regarding his greater interest in trade rather than aid. In reality, Wade wanted more and more aid. Senegal's political success needed to be reinforced by economic success. For months after Wade's election, the international press lauded Senegal for transparent and fair elections. If only the much-needed improvements in education and health care could have merited similar coverage.

When Wade broke his pledge not to seek a third term, he almost destroyed Senegal's reputation as a star performer in sub-Saharan politics. However, Macky Sall, a former prime minister, defeated President Wade in April 2012.

Senegal has retained a multiparty system since its independence in 1960. The U.S. government provides direct financial assistance each year, mainly in the form of supporting good governance. Senegal was one of the first participants in the African Crisis Response Initiative, which under the Bush administration in 2004 became the African Contingency Operations Training and Assistance Program; it promotes joint training exercises among African forces to help them better respond to emergencies.

During the Clinton administration, the U.S. government helped establish the African Center for Strategic Studies in Dakar. It has become the preeminent Department of Defense institution for strategic security studies, research, and outreach in Africa. A peace and security forum in late 2014 brought together security professionals from Africa, Europe, Asia, and the United States to respond during times of crisis. And during the recent Ebola outbreak, Senegal became the staging area for the health clinic buildings being constructed in Liberia.

Even the social life of an ambassador can be all business. I used to give up wine for Lent. One year, while dining at the home of Babette Ndiaye, chief of the Central Bank of West Africa's antilaundering operations, I noticed that the Catholic bishop was drinking wine during Lent. I was envious because I was counting the days until the end of Lent. Inevitably, the French ambassador's dinner party during Lent served the best French wines and champagne. I used all my willpower to drink only Perrier water.

For my entire diplomatic career, and certainly as ambassador, I had to remain serious at receptions, dinners, and many other formal occasions. It was not a burden. I enjoyed my duties. I smile when I remember how the late John Gravely, a very dear friend, teased me about my joy in attending and greeting guests at receptions, ceremonies, concerts, and performances. I guess that comes from having been a cultural attaché and a diplomat for much of my life. I was not surprised when, at the end of a performance of the Boys' Choir of Harlem at the Kennedy Center, John said, "Harriet has not seen a receiving line she could refuse."

Formal events in Dakar were no different. And of course, Wilfred and I could never stay late. If we did not leave, the other guests who understood protocol could not leave. Occasionally, we attended events at one of the Americans' homes. One Thanksgiving we went to the USAID director Don Clark's home. Don was one of the few Americans comfortable, and not pretentious, wearing a traditional African grand *boubou*. He looked great. The turkey dinner was so tasty, I wanted to take a little with me, but Wilfred was insistent. I could not ask for a doggy bag. He said it was inappropriate for an ambassador to make such a request.

About eleven o'clock he nudged me about leaving, but first I slipped into the kitchen and asked if I could get a little of the turkey and dressing to take home. Connie fixed me up a little package with a whisper of another little secret. Wilfred had made his own request for some of the spicy pepper sauce! It was in these small, yet important, ways that Connie touched the heart and soul of the embassy community.

She invited me to a sort of bridal shower to see the interesting traditions that take place prior to a wedding. I will admit, I thought most traditional cultures were extremely conservative, since most women were covered from head to toe in the grand *boubous*. Well, I learned that assumption was incorrect. At the shower, we were able to witness what the bride wears under the wedding dress. What we saw would make Victoria Secret's bestsellers pale in comparison! And that's all I'm saying. It was thanks to Connie Clark that many embassy employees learned Senegalese rituals and events that were invaluable as we built credible relationships. Connie was a master at cross-cultural communication. In many ways, she was our informal ambassador.

Wilfred and I traveled to South Africa in November 2001 to visit a number of my colleagues posted in Johannesburg, Durban, and Cape Town. After having traveled to South Africa in 1998 as counselor of the USIA, I wanted to see what had transpired since the end of apartheid. We thought it wise to make the trip while on the continent, for it was less likely that we would travel that distance from the United States.

At our stop in Durban, a coastal city in South Africa, we were the guests of Amelia Broderick, then branch public affairs officer in Durban. One afternoon we visited her offices in the U.S. consulate as she briefed a group of South African librarians selected as international visitors under the State Department's Educational and Cultural Exchange Program. They were going to spend four weeks in the United States, meeting with American librarians and sharing their expertise with one another. This program, which continues, provides international visitors opportunities to correct misperceptions about the United States and allows for significant cross-cultural communication as they share the latest techniques of their professions. Since their trip was to begin only two months after the tragedy of September 11, the librarians were understandably apprehensive. Actually, to be candid, they were really frightened. As Amelia gave her briefing, I listened to her calming their fears while acknowledging their concerns. She explained the program's content and goals and the counterparts they would meet. One of the highlights of their visit would be a trip to the Library of Congress and possibly a meeting with the respected librarian of Congress, Dr. James Billington. They left comforted, informed, and excited about going. I said to Amelia, "You learned your lessons well." I told her she could have been justifiably skeptical about sending international visitors to the United States at that point, but she never showed it. She provided relevant information, including alerting them to the heightened security at airports. She calmed their fears without painting an unrealistic picture of what to expect in the United States. I was extremely proud of her.

For the Fourth of July 2002, Wilfred and I hosted the last of our Independence Day receptions at the ambassador's residence in

Senegal. American ambassadors invite the diplomatic corps, senior host government officials, business leaders, educators, journalists, and nongovernmental organization (NGO) representatives to this event. It is a highly sought-after invitation for those who like to have "face time" with dignitaries. Each year ambassadors try to offer entertainment unique to America. Given America's diversity and the wealth of traditional art performances that represent that diversity, we were delighted with our artistic offering that year. We welcomed the Cultural Academy for Excellence's Positive Vibrations Youth Steel Orchestra for its first performance in Africa. CAFE, as the music program also is known, is based in the Greater Washington city of Hyattsville, Maryland.

For more than a year, my husband, working with our public affairs officer, Michael Pelletier, had been trying to secure funding to bring the seventeen young musicians of the steel pan to Senegal. The steel pan originated in Trinidad. It is what my husband rightly calls Trinidad's gift to the world. After the September 11 attacks, the public affairs officer knew of Washington's desire to counter the influence of fundamentalist imams who might seek to radicalize youth throughout Senegal. He crafted a winning proposal to the Department of State to bring the young steel pan performers to play for us. The young men and women were not only masterful musicians, but at their very young age, they were effective communicators on TV and in person. The youngest one was about ten years old. This little girl charmed the interviewer so much that he gave her more time to speak than the older pan artists. What a joy she was to watch.

All CAFE members are American citizens from families of Caribbean origin. They were disciplined. They came from a tradition where parents did not suffer fools. When they performed, they captured the hearts and minds of the guests.

They played not only calypso and soca, which is the typical musical idiom of Trinidad and Tobago, but also classical compositions. They must know and be able to read all music genres. They do not play by ear. Their versatility has brought them numerous national prizes in steel pan competitions. They are serious and gifted musicians.

My "diplomat" husband understood the importance of national anthems. He sent the music of Senegal's national anthem to the director of CAFE. They mastered it. The orchestra played both the U.S. and the Senegalese national anthems at the beginning of the Fourth of July reception before our twelve hundred guests. Senegal's minister of defense spoke with me immediately after the formal speeches and said it was the most beautiful rendition of his country's national anthem he had ever heard. The Tunisian ambassador commented, "We had been confronted with so much negativism from the media, we needed this uplift." Once again, I was witness to the positive role of the arts in diplomacy. The Tunisian ambassador invited the CAFE founder and director, Lorna Green, to his office and presented her with a ceramic tree of life, a symbol that alludes to the interconnection of all life on our planet and serves as a metaphor for common descent in the evolutionary sense that is known in many cultures. I have seen that tree displayed along with the myriad of awards and trophies at the Hyattsville headquarters of CAFE.

The band members also performed at an outdoor concert along the Atlantic Ocean at the Porte du Millénaire (Door of the Millennium), a sculpture designed by Senegalese architect Pierre Goudiaby Atepa. It is along the Grande Corniche, also known as Martin Luther King Boulevard. The sculpture was completed in 2001 as Africa's tribute to the new millennium, with symbolism representing unity and communication between the diverse cultures of Africa. It is a popular entertainment venue, but since it is outdoors, I was told by my security detail I could not go. I would be too exposed. Now, having married a Trinidadian and having seen how hard he and my staff worked to get this group to Dakar, I wanted to see the performers somewhere other than the ambassador's residence. The regional security officer insisted that I ride in an armored vehicle similar to a Hummer. I was told to remain inside the vehicle to listen to the performance. From our parking spot, I could barely see. I persuaded my bodyguard to let me exit the vehicle and walk a bit closer. He accompanied me to the perimeter of the stage. Music historians trace the rhythms of calypso to the French sugarcane planters who brought West African slaves to the Caribbean islands in the 1700s. That made another wonderful cross-cultural tie in terms of the drum in the traditional African culture and the Caribbean culture, and then spread to the world. It was wonderful to behold.

At the State Department's invitation, Lorna Green returned to Senegal to conduct workshops with NGOs working with young men and women in two provincial villages. Again, this was a concerted effort to mount a counteroffensive to the potential negative influence of fundamentalist Muslims on Senegalese youth. One of the participants in the workshop was a Professor Diagne from St. Louis University in Senegal's first capital city, Saint Louis (the capital was moved to Dakar in 1902). He also was so impressed that he invited Lorna Green to conduct workshops during the annual summer camp sessions in Senegal's first capital. Clearly music and the arts are effective in bridging cultural divides and in exposing young people to a less conflicted world. Yes, my husband was very proud, and I was very proud that he soldiered on in this effort.

10

I Was Ready to Retire . . . I Thought

Everyone is familiar with the title "ambassador," and many people think they know what the job entails. Most of those impressions are wrong, however. Few people have any idea who gets the title or what that person really does. And . . . whether they are necessary at all. —DENNIS JETT, *American Ambassadors*

I did not seek out what has become my final Foreign Service assignment, becoming the first diplomat in residence at the University of Central Florida. I was ready to retire. I thought. Ambassador Ruth A. Davis, who had rallied after a major health challenge, called me and said, "Harriet, we need to have more women and minorities in this business. I am convinced that I'm on the planet because there's still work for me to do." She began her career in 1969, when white, Ivy League–educated men dominated the diplomatic field. In 2001 she was sworn in as director general of the Foreign Service after having directed the Foreign Service Institute, the State Department's university-like training complex in Arlington, Virginia. It was impossible for me to say no to this respected senior diplomat and colleague who, at that time, was the highest-ranking African American woman in the State Department. (Condoleezza Rice became secretary of state in 2005.) Ambassador Davis, my very close friend and advisor, remains a role model for scores of other women as the only woman to date with the rank of career ambassador, equivalent to a four-star general.

I agreed to take on this new task for the 2003–4 academic year. At the threshold of the very end of my professional career, I took on this new role with the same excitement I felt with all of my assignments. To date, I have not regretted this decision. My new home was UCF's Office of Global Perspectives, headed by a Pulitzer Prize–winning journalist, John Bersia. He was totally committed to implementing UCF president John Hitt's vision to ensure the University of Central Florida (and by extension, the Central Florida region) was globally connected. Through the president's efforts this university is partnered with 182 other institutions and universities, many of them based abroad.

My new role came with some nonacademic responsibilities. In August 2003 the White House notified me that I had been selected to read the president's message to the nation at a ceremony at Orlando's Lake Eola to mark the second anniversary of the September 11 terrorist attacks. We were still new to the region and living about an hour's drive away, in Leesburg. We got lost on our drive to downtown Orlando, and the event coordinator sent a police escort to lead us. As we arrived, I heard the Orlando Philharmonic playing American composer Aaron Copland's best-known concert opener, "Fanfare for the Common Man." I was moved by the music, which was truly appropriate for the president's message. Later, when I went to compliment the orchestra, I met Mark Fischer, one of the founding members and principal horn since 1996. He had identified himself as "just a French horn player." I told him to never use that qualifier. I also told him that as a cultural attaché for so many years, I had come to appreciate all kinds of music. He introduced me to David Schillhammer, the executive director.

A short time later, I was asked to narrate Copland's *Lincoln Portrait*. Written during World War II to promote American patriotism, it incoporates excerpts from the Gettysburg Address and other Lincoln speeches and writings. I was honored to join the many celebrities and political leaders who have read the narration with a full orchestra. Somewhat overwhelmed to have this opportunity, I prepared by listening to many other narrators, including James Earl Jones, and I tried to lower my voice. UCF Theater Department chair Roberta Sloan told me to stop trying to sound like someone else, use my own solemn voice, and let Lincoln's words speak for themselves. Copland had written very similar instructions for the simple, direct narration, cautioning against attempts to make Lincoln's words overly dramatic. "The words are sufficiently dramatic in themselves; they need no added 'emotion' in order to put them across to an audience," he wrote. No recordings exist of Lincoln's voice, but Smithsonian historians note that Lincoln was a tenor. Crowds had no trouble hearing Lincoln's voice carry, but he spoke with a higher, perhaps shriller pitch than many of the other noted orators of his time, and certainly not with the voice of James Earl Jones.

When the day of the event arrived, I was with several friends and classmates from Boston, Washington, and Atlanta, including my brother and his wife, some ten out-of-towners altogether. We were all backstage and the woman who became my closest friend in Florida, Beverly Marshall-Luney, then the vice president of investment and governmental affairs for the Metropolitan Orlando Economic Development Commission, decided I didn't have enough makeup on, and I was wearing the wrong kind of earrings. She put every bit of makeup she had in her purse on my face and then took her earrings off and put them on me. She made me look dazzling. As a conservative diplomat, I usually wear black, navy, or gray. Here I was looking like what I thought was a kabuki dancer with red lipstick, heavy eyeliner, and these glimmering earrings, but from the stage, it was just right. For thirteen minutes I sat on a stool before saying a word as the orchestra performed. Then I got the high sign from Maestro Hal France, and I was on. I was absolutely over the moon, as I later told Linda Chapin. She nonchalantly commented, "Oh, I did that years ago."

I had met Linda, a political activist and civil rights icon in this community, within the last two days of my arrival at the UCF campus. As I entered the Global Perspectives conference room for my initial meeting with John Bersia, I noticed signed black and white photographs gracing the walls. Unlike the walls of the hallways of the State Department, which are often decorated with historic images or recent travel photos of the secretary of state, these were pictures with signatures and collectibles of women who had made distinctive differences in this world: Eleanor Roosevelt, Shirley Chisholm,

Margaret Thatcher, Rosa Parks, Sally Ride, Mary McLeod Bethune, Helen Keller, Golda Meir, Katharine Graham, and others. What a wonderful setting in which to work. I was elated just to know that somebody cared enough to put together this wonderful collection. John immediately said that the display did not belong to the university. The framed portraits belonged to Linda Chapin.

In 1990 Linda became the Orange County Commission's first chairman elected by a countywide vote. She had earned great political capital by persuading the Walt Disney Company to buy the county's housing finance authority's bonds and to provide mortgage assistance to lower- and middle-income families. Chapin, winner of the 2004 James B. Greene Award given by the Metro Orlando Economic Development Commission for significant contributions to the region's economic growth, continued to influence public policy when in 2001 she became director of the Metropolitan Center for Regional Studies at UCF. After I'd been here a while and we had collaborated, Linda came to my office one day. She said, "Harriet, have you ever attended one of the executive leadership programs at the Kennedy School of Government?" I had not.

Linda arranged for the two of us to attend a weeklong Women in Leadership seminar through the Executive Education Program at the John F. Kennedy School of Government at Harvard University. The Kennedy School describes itself as "the vanguard of studying public policy and preparing its practitioners." The seminar exceeded our expectations. We were with fifty-two women from around the United States and six from overseas, all women who had done significant things in their lives. Harvard professors doing research on conflict regions of the world interviewed them. Linda and I persuaded the Kennedy School coordinator to schedule a morning session with these six global women. It was the most riveting, most enlightening time of the entire week. They described their greatest challenges and accomplishments in their positions. While I had lived and worked overseas for thirty-five years, I told Linda I would be forever in her debt for creating this opportunity for me to interact with these extraordinary women.

Linda invited my husband and me to her home for our first Thanksgiving in Orlando. I was very fortunate to have had those couple of years working with Linda. It truly opened my eyes to what civic activism could do below the Mason-Dixon line.

The first year at UCF turned out to be a very satisfying assignment. At first, many of the young men and women I encountered had no clue about Foreign Service careers or the Department of State. Many became genuinely interested in a host of globally focused careers.

Upon my arrival, I met with all of the UCF deans. In one instance, the dean of the College of Business, Thomas Keon, now chancellor at Purdue University Calumet, insisted that he should come to my office to meet with me. During that meeting I learned of his keen interest in global affairs and that his senior administrative assistant just happened to be Anne Marie de Govia, originally from Trinidad, the director of UCF's Caribbean Students Organization for twenty years. Given her leadership and the Caribbean parents' focus on academic achievement, it is no wonder that the majority of students of color competitive for Pickering and Rangel Fellowships had Caribbean origins.

I addressed faculty lunches and Rotary clubs, visited career resource centers, and met with the presidents of private colleges and community colleges in the Central Florida region. Each encounter led to genuine commitments from certain members of these groups to help the university achieve its goals, evidenced by increased numbers of students studying abroad.

As I gave presentations on Foreign Service careers, I became UCF's Pied Piper for students interested in international affairs. Students had been told an ambassador was coming, "but we didn't think it would be you," as one student phrased what became typical of surprised observations. I did not fit the usual image. I was not a middle-aged, gray-haired gent sporting a pinstriped suit with a boutonniere in his lapel.

In classroom lectures, I addressed the multifaceted Foreign Service career and provided a personal testimony on the pros and cons of diplomatic life. After speaking to hundreds of students at career fairs, information sessions, and individual meetings, I noticed an increase in the well-crafted questions students posed. They were really interested in a career they knew little about before my arrival at UCF. In several instances, the parents had encouraged their children to follow well-known career tracks to become lawyers, doctors, marketing experts, IT experts, and entrepreneurs. Parents and students wondered, What would one do with a degree in international relations? What did diplomats really do? Was this a profession where the parents could see a tangible return on their investment?

Students kept coming to my office for information or to request permission to enroll in the diplomacy course. Since I taught in the Honors College, the class size was limited to twenty. Additional students would need an "override" from the professor to attend. One of UCF's most respected and longtime professors and a former dean, Dr. Robert Bledsoe, who currently teaches international law and related courses, said, "Since you have been here, I have more students interested in pursuing a career in international affairs."

Faculty advisors and Dr. Alvin Wang, dean of Burnett Honors College, are justifiably proud that their students are competitive with those of the Ivy League institutions for the State Department's prestigious Pickering and Rangel Fellowships.

Dr. Bledsoe and Dr. Wang have sent many students to meet with me. At Dr. Wang's request, I have served on several mock interview panels for students who reached the interview process for prestigious awards. As I participated in those panels, I was reminded of the "murder board" that I went through prior to my Senate confirmation hearings. Our questions were often more challenging than those the students would receive at their interviews. We wanted to be sure they were well prepared.

When I have doubts about the value of my work at UCF, I need only to remember my students who went on to the London School of Economics or Kent University in England or those who received State Department Critical Language Scholarships and Boren, Rangel, and Pickering Fellowships for graduate studies. Those last two fellowships include a five-year commitment to work at the State Department. Others have spent a year teaching English in China and South Korea or joined the Peace Corps and served in Cambodia or worked for humanitarian NGOs in Colombia. Others have received scholarships to study abroad in Taiwan and been involved in service-learning projects in St. Kitts–Nevis and South Africa. One has been the recipient of a Clinton Global Initiative Grant, which allowed him to return to St. Kitts upon his 2015 UCF graduation for a year to complete the work he began on a sustainable development project. As I watch their progress and continued enthusiasm about global affairs, I am encouraged to continue this work. Their handwritten thank you letters and their emails have confirmed my optimism about America's next leaders. One student noted, "As a student at UCF, I have attended several career fairs, and yours was the first to have a lasting impression on me. Instead of packing up at the end of the fair, you had us huddle in a group and took the time to explain how each of us could be an asset." One student representative at the Model UN conference held at Bethune-Cookman College, a historically black college in Daytona Beach, told me my closing remarks gave him precisely the argument needed for him to win his country's position in the "mock vote," which took place immediately following my presentation. That student has stayed in touch with me and has traveled to Orlando to further his research on a Foreign Service career.

As the title implies, diplomats in residence are career Foreign Service officers on campuses throughout the United States who provide students and professionals with guidance and advice on careers, internships, and fellowships. With more than sixty-four thousand students, many of international origin, UCF is fertile ground for a well focused Foreign Service recruitment effort. I welcomed the challenge to broaden their perspectives of the world and to encourage them to consider careers abroad. Central Florida also has become home to individuals who speak many languages and who understand America's cultural and societal challenges. I tapped into this resource to heighten the students' international focus and widened the prism through which the broader Orlando community viewed the U.S. diplomatic service.

The diplomat in residence program was established to reach students who ordinarily might not be aware of the work of diplomats. The program is not offered at Ivy League universities and mainstream universities. Rather, these career diplomats are assigned to campuses with significant populations of minorities, women, and Native Americans and to schools in "middle America," such as the University of Oklahoma, the University of Santa Fe, and certainly universities in Florida. We need to gain a perspective from individuals who are less conversant with international issues. Historically, the majority of U.S. diplomatic corps has been made up of graduates from a Ivy League schools. They bring only the perspective of an elite, privileged group. Even if the Ivy Leaguers have gained their education through scholarships, not legacy, they have been imbued with a sense of how "special" they are. That privilege can be a detriment to gaining credibility with one's counterparts abroad. More recently the Department of State has included men and women who come from all parts of the United States. There are, however, very few Native Americans in the Foreign Service. In my forty-two-year career, I have met and worked with only two. The diplomat in residence program informs students of their potential to represent the United States abroad, and they bring a much-needed diverse perspective to the Department of State's work.

In today's working world, we interact with individuals from Asia, Africa, Latin America, and the newly independent states of the former Soviet Union. What better way to be more effective than to incorporate the perspective of someone who has not already felt that he or she was privileged?

The diplomat in residence program provides much-needed information to communities around the nation that are ill informed about the U.S. Foreign Service. The same enthusiasm and motivation a career diplomat needs to articulate U.S. policy, culture, and society to audiences abroad are now shared with domestic audiences. This new role has been most gratifying.

I completed my first year in the Office of Global Perspectives with incredible support from my colleagues, Ambassadors Ulric Haynes,

Gary Grappo, and Myles Frechette. All of them have addressed our students. Ulric Haynes kept the students in rapt attention as he recounted how he persuaded the Algerian government to assist in the U.S.-Iranian negotiations that resulted in the January 1980 release of the U.S. embassy hostages in Iran. Of Barbadian origin and a successful former businessman and former dean of the School of Business and executive dean for international relations at Hofstra University, Ambassador Haynes is a vivid example of the importance of diversity in making effective foreign policy. Ambassador Grappo was equally riveting each time he spoke of his work when ambassador to Oman and as a member of the Mission for the Quartet Representatives in Jerusalem. Ambassador Myles Frechette provided invaluable insight on our often-overlooked neighbors in Latin America. I look forward to his UCF visits, and even now, I am enthralled listening to his stories of life in the Foreign Service, particularly about his time as ambassador to Colombia. He received the State Department's Distinguished Service Award for his superb performance in one of the most difficult assignments in the Foreign Service, Colombia. He and his family lived under constant, real threats from Colombian narcotics traffickers and guerrillas. UCF students are fortunate to have these highly respected professionals in their midst, and I am honored to be among their colleagues.

I frequently remind students that the U.S. Foreign Service is a far more inclusive government agency than it was in the early years of my career, but it still needs more women and minorities. I also highlight the importance of inclusion of male graduates from all of America's diverse colleges and universities. I catch their attention when I speak at an information session by saying, "I do not want all the white males in this room to leave this setting. We need individuals of all hues who come from different parts of the United States not traditionally represented in the U.S. diplomatic service. That means all of you!" (I did not want to lose my audience. Although DIRs are encouraged to recruit women and minorities, recruiting first-generation college goers of all races and genders is important if the State Department is to represent America.) Instantly, the skepticism disappears, and

I continue my presentation. Of the three UCF Pickering fellows to date, two were not minorities, and one was a first-generation college graduate.

Sarah Maarti, a 2015 Rangel fellow who was one of my diplomacy students, returned to speak to one of my classes after four years as a career FSO. She gave a fascinating chronicle of her life in her first two posts. She spoke about her increasingly substantive work experiences and the relationships she made. She added that only her engagement prompted her to leave the Foreign Service. Sarah kept in touch with me and with Martha Hitt, Dr. John Hitt's wife, for many months during her first overseas tour. She has established a scholarship in her name at UCF.

After the first year, I was ready to leave UCF. Dr. Hitt's letter to the State Department brought approval for me to stay for a second year. I am certain my host, John Bersia, encouraged Dr. Hitt to send this message, and I shall be forever grateful for John's foresight. At the end of my second year, I reached the required retirement age for all career Foreign Service officers. In September 2005 I retired from the U.S. Senior Foreign Service with the rank of career minister, the equivalent of a three-star general in the military. President Hitt asked me to remain on campus to establish a Diplomacy Program. In 2007 UCF received approval from Tallahassee for a "Diplomacy Certificate" program, and I began to teach. (Since 2013, students have been able to receive a minor in the field of diplomacy through the Political Science Department.)

Also in 2007, my undergrad alma mater, Simmons College, asked if I would host one of its Afghan students for a weeklong visit to Orlando. Simmons's Mosaic Program promotes international diversity and pairs students with those in their future professions. Adela Raz was that student. After her graduation from Simmons, she gained her master's from my other alma mater, the Fletcher School. I met with her twice while she was in DC working for an NGO before she returned to Afghanistan. Adela became a leading advocate for gender equality, women's education, human rights, governance, and political affairs. She continues to hold a senior post in the Afghan government.

During her UCF visit, she shadowed my work each day. Adela joined me as I was part of a panel interviewing UCF candidates for the prestigious President's Leadership Council (PLC), where she observed the best and the brightest at UCF. Members of the PLC council attend board meetings, and they also serve as hosts at graduations and as representatives of UCF at events outside the university. They must be discreet. They cannot share what they learn in board meetings and in other high-level meetings at the university. I have addressed three or four of the new councils since my arrival at UCF. These are extraordinary young men and women.

After the PLC interviews, Adela joined me for an event held by my sorority, Delta Sigma Theta, for a session entitled "I Am Not My Hair." The event, organized to prepare students for their professional lives, has been offered on campuses across the nation. In 2005 India Arie released a single with the same title, drawn from the writings of a Persian poet and theologian often identified as Rumi, who died in 1273. His poems, including the quote that inspired the song—"I am not this hair. I am not this skin. I am the soul that lives within"—have been widely translated.

I was invited to speak at the event because of my work on campus. Yet I have no doubt that my hair, my silver braids pulled back in what my niece Patricia describes as resembling intricately woven African basket designs, had something to do with the invitation. I talked about how often first impressions are made by hairstyles. It does not matter what color you are, it is how your hair is coiffed. It makes a statement. I was delighted to share some of the background of this coiffure that goes back thousands of years.

My decision to wear this hairstyle dates from 1988 and the first African American Alumnae Symposium at Simmons. There were 167 women of color in the room, many of them graduates of the Simmons Graduate School of Management. The undergraduate school never had more than a handful of African American students each year until the 1970s. My class had only four African American students. There were only two in the class before me, and one in the senior class. By the 1970s there were maybe twenty-five. Some of them had begun wearing Afros and joined the demonstrators who filed into the president's office to demand the college hire more black faculty members. Some of the same women's careers landed them on the covers of *Fortune* magazine. None of them have Afros anymore. I had an Afro for about twenty-four hours when I was a junior in college. That was just something my parents were not going to allow me to do.

The keynote speaker at the alumnae symposium was Susan Taylor, then editor in chief of *Essence* magazine. She was absolutely stunning, with a beautiful bronze complexion, a high forehead, and her hair styled with pageboy braids. To this day, she wears the same hairstyle. She readily gave me the name of her braider in New York City, Elin LaVar, whose clients have included Dionne Warwick, Oprah Winfrey, and a host of other celebrities. I admire Susan Taylor, for many women in the public arena do not share such information with others. When I learned the price of the braids would be $500, I cringed. I knew my 1988 State Department salary would not allow me to make such an investment, so I dipped into my savings account. I traveled from Washington to New York and stayed with my friends Kathy and Arthur Stewart on Staten Island. They accompanied me on the ferry to Manhattan for an appointment that would change my look for the rest of my life.

I sat in Elin LaVar's chair for eight hours as she braided my hair. I came out a new person. The braids had a subtle dignity about them. All of a sudden, I felt comfortable in my own skin. I wasn't the diplomat who is black trying to be white.

I really did not know how the State Department would react. I did not have to wait long. I attended William Swing's swearing in as ambassador to Liberia a few days after I returned from New York with my new braids. He said to me, "Harriet—Ah—Cleopatra." I responded, "Nefertiti would be more appropriate."

I really feel Susan was central to my accepting who I was as a person of color in the diplomatic service. I no longer had to toe the line of being unnoticeable. In many ways, that was a powerful identity statement. Yes, I was aware that some of the corporate and government leadership and some of my colleagues frowned upon and even prohibited their staff from wearing braids, no matter how neat they were. They viewed it as a political statement, a challenge, and perhaps it was. Thankfully, that is no longer the case. At the time, however, I was proud of my heritage, even if it meant I would always have to prove I was equal to, if not better prepared than, my white diplomatic colleagues.

While I wanted to return to Elin LaVar, I knew I could not afford that price again. Fortunately, Kai DeRosa, a young woman of Cape Verdean descent in Washington DC, did a superb job of matching Elin LaVar's expertise. I relied on Kai for the counsel she gave to my braiders when I was posted in Brussels. My hairstyle has changed. It's still in braids, but it is no longer in the pageboy style. In Brussels I started pulling it back, braided into a style similar to a French twist. I just couldn't be bothered with a bad hair day!

Through the years, I have found other braiders. Several months after my husband and I took up residence in Leesburg, I met Gnil Toure, a delightful young Senegalese entrepreneur. She has been doing my hair ever since. My husband and I were honored to attend her citizenship ceremony in mid-May 2015 at the Orlando Office of Immigration and Naturalization Services.

At Delta Sigma Theta's "I Am Not My Hair" event, I recognized that I was in a room with some three hundred African American students, probably the most I had seen in one place in my three years on campus. I introduced them to my guest from Afghanistan, Adela Raz, who was wearing a traditional headscarf, but otherwise western dress. I explained she was visiting the campus as part of Simmons's program that encourages all foreign students to shadow someone in a profession close to the one they hope to follow. I then shared with them that she had a 3.9 GPA with a triple major in international relations, political science, and economics. (She would go on to graduate with honors in 2008, then earn a master's degree in law and diplomacy from the Fletcher School at Tufts University.) When I added that English was not her first language, all of a sudden I heard this "ah," as if all the oxygen had been sucked out of the room. I realized I had the audience. They no longer cared about hair. It was the fact that I had this student from Afghanistan who was fluent in her native Pashtun and Dari as well as Urdu and some Arabic. I spoke a bit about her journey. The Taliban had killed her father because he was perceived as too progressive. She had been the first Afghan to gain a HIBI visa (for foreign workers in specialty occupations) from the consular section of the U.S. embassy in Kabul, and then-ambassador E. Anthony Wayne made the presentation. She was studying to become involved in international affairs as a representative in humanitarian assistance with an NGO. Yes, this woman was not her hair!

I believe that something positive happened during Adela's experiences in the United States. She was determined, she was committed, and she made it her duty to represent her county well. She has subsequently worked to promote economic development in Afghanistan, assist Afghan widows, and help women develop sustainable livelihoods and participate in Afghan society. She has been recognized for her comprehensive experience in the fields of human rights, governance, and political affairs. In 2013 she was named first deputy spokesperson and director of communications for Afghanistan, the first woman to hold the post as official spokesperson for then-president Hamid Karzai. She continues to work for President Ashraf Ghani Ahmadzai. At this writing, she was the foreign minister for economic relations.

Adela Raz is an exceptional woman, but she is not unique. In 2009 I traveled to the World Innovation Summit for Educators at Doha, the capital city of Qatar. The capital's Education City includes early education facilities as well as higher education research campuses and branches of many foreign universities. All the college women, dressed in black, were studying economics and finance. I kept wondering, where are they going to use their education? Students from around the world made presentations. They represented Harvard, Yale, and the universities of England. A United Arab Emirates student, dressed from head to toe in black, told the history of her country and what it meant for women to be educated. She knocked it out of the park. She had been coached by an English teacher from the United States, who taught her how to connect with her audience.

She had presentation skills down. I just hope she will be able to use them in a society that doesn't seem to have a lot for women to do. There is one thing I observed in that oil-rich part of the world: the population does not seem to work. The workforce is overwhelmingly composed of expatriates from Pakistan, the Philippines, or somewhere else. There are no indigenous workers in the high-end stores or hotels. I do not know what they were training these women for. But it did tell me the country's young leadership is a knowledge-based cadre. They want to remove the stigma of women not being at the fore. How much they have succeeded in that, I do not know.

I spent a third year at UCF, and again, I am certain the appointment came due to John Bersia's recommendation. I gave the commencement address at one of UCF's five commencements that year. I was absolutely thrilled to learn that I was the recipient of an honorary doctorate from UCF. Before the actual ceremony, I had received several emails inviting me to attend a board of trustees meeting. I went out of sheer curiosity. I was totally surprised when they announced I was among the three honorary doctoral degree recipients that year. I was surprised because in my brief acceptance remarks I said, "It has been my honor to show the UCF students and the Central Florida region there is a world beyond Disney and Universal." How undiplomatic! Both of those institutions are the largest employers in this area. And to make matters even worse, the chairmen of UCF's board of trustees at that time was none other than the CEO of Disney World. As I looked around the huge table, I spotted him and quickly crafted a second sentence, which did not cast aspersions on the economic engine of this region. Whew!

My work in the Office of Global Perspectives and my collaboration with John Bersia on a host of the international initiatives he has launched have been enlightening, gratifying, and reassuring.

In August 2008 the Orlando Economic Development Commission (EDC) sent its first overseas trade delegation to Montreal. Its vice president for investor relations, Beverly Marshall-Luney, asked me to join the delegation. The EDC's goal was to strengthen international ties and to study Canada's rapid transportation system and its creative approach to homelessness, health care, and the performing arts. After briefing the senior EDC officers, I studied my brief and then reconnected with a former protégé who had become consul general in Montreal and gave a reception for the mayor of Orlando and our eighty-eight-member delegation.

I have met with university administrators from Croatia for three consecutive years and from Sweden twice. The Global Perspectives Office's partnership with universities in northern Iraq/Kurdistan provided opportunities to meet with their delegations. Memberships on advisory boards of the Middle East Program and the Isle of Man Small Countries Program have allowed me to interact with senior officials and scholars from those regions. I could not have landed in a more magnificent setting to keep my global connections alive and well.

UCF now has four Pickering fellows, three of whom won the prestigious fellowship since my arrival on campus. The university also has a second Rangel fellow, Nicholas Grandchamps, another former diplomacy student who received his master's degree from American University and will enter the State Department's fall 2017 A100 course (the six-month training course for new FSOs.)

Several of my students have taken and passed the written Foreign Service officer test. Although some are still challenged by the next entry requirement—the Qualifications Evaluation Panel segment—we are truly proud of those who were successful in passing the written exam.

Florida now has diplomats in residence in Tallahassee at Florida A&M University, which serves Central and North Florida as well as the southern portions of Georgia, Alabama, and Mississippi, and in Miami at Florida International University/Miami Dade College. All of the DIRs have been dynamic. I have attended several of their UCF presentations. They have made use of the latest technology so well that even I, a retiree, was excited about the new U.S. Foreign Service.

This nation has embraced one of its greatest assets: a multicultural citizenry that truly reflects the world in which we live. My work in Central Florida has included addresses to international economic summits, UN-related programs, Rotary clubs, U.S. Army War College National Strategic Exercises, chamber of commerce galas, UCF leadership training institutes, and numerous panels. In each instance, I believe my presence delivers a subtle yet profound message that even I could become a successful diplomat, speak four languages, and carry on a meaningful dialogue with the most senior ranks in the U.S. and foreign governments.

My life has come a long way from the surprise child brought up by loving and supportive parents and very supportive siblings who played major roles in getting me to this point. I have no children of my own, but I have sixteen nieces and nephews and handfuls of grand-nieces and nephews. On October 3, 1999, when I married Wilfred Thomas, I inherited four stepchildren and five more grandchildren.

At my seventieth birthday roast at the Marriott hotel on the campus of the University of Maryland, one of my nieces, Patricia, and my nephew Jay, now both senior citizens, although their personas and creativity defy the more traditional view of a senior, entertained the guests with embellished stories of the times I took care of them when they were young children. Apparently, they thought I was strict, too strict, when I was their babysitter. They let their parents know that I was not their babysitter of choice. "She was mean," they told this gathering of people who only know me as the polite diplomat. They went on and on about how I would not let them play outside with their friends after dark or let them eat and drink what and when they wanted. One, Patricia Elam-Walker, is now a published novelist and former assistant director of the Center for Excellence in Teaching at Simmons College. In the fall of 2015 she returned to Howard University as a professor of creative writing. The other, Dr. Harry J. Elam Jr., is vice president for the arts and currently vice provost at Stanford University. Both are creative and know a bit about theatrics. The audience couldn't stop laughing. I do not think anybody remembers anything else from that night, except for Rhoda Scott's unbelievable mastery of the Hammond organ. I just happened to be the birthday girl—no longer the "little Elam girl" and now an acknowledged "senior" citizen.

One year earlier, in 2010, I received the *Onyx* magazine Global Award in Central Florida. Several students reflected on my impact on their lives in video interviews. In their own fashion, they acknowledged that there is a world beyond the United States, and they want to be actively engaged in its future. I cherish those interviews.

Epilogue

Coming Full Circle, Cuba Face-to-Face

Today, I can announce that the United States has agreed to formally reestablish diplomatic relations with the Republic of Cuba and reopen embassies in our respective countries. This is a historic step forward in our efforts to normalize relations with the Cuban government and people and begin a new chapter with our neighbors in the Americas. —PRESIDENT BARACK OBAMA, July 1, 2015

On July 1, 2015, President Barack Obama walked from the steps outside the Oval Office at the West Wing of the White House and stood at a podium in the Rose Garden to tell the nation of his plans to reopen the U.S. embassy in Havana, which President Dwight Eisenhower had closed fifty-four years before. That same Wednesday morning, the seventh day of my educational and cultural exchange visit to Cuba, I awoke at the 1930s Hotel Nacional de Cuba in central Havana's Vedado district, with its hillside view of the city's harbor. My fourth-floor room was not one of the hotel's celebrity-named rooms but was between the ones named for Buster Keaton and Walt Disney. Next time, I'll ask for Nat King Cole's room.

When Fulgencio Batista took command of the Cuban army in 1933, the art deco–influenced hotel was the scene of an eleven-hour gunfight between army officers who refused to recognize Batista's authority and soldiers loyal to the coup. The hotel had been the temporary residence of U.S. ambassador Sumner Welles, who left before the shooting started. Later, mobsters Santos Traficante and Meyer Lansky met with Batista at the hotel to negotiate their casinos. The hotel is now a UNESCO World Heritage Site, but that morning I prepared to visit a far more significant historic landmark in U.S.-Cuba relations.

By midmorning I was sitting with my fourteen-member tour group in the sterile briefing room of the U.S. Interests Section (the same building that nineteen days later once again became an embassy). Our briefer had been called out by another staffer. Moments later, the sound of applause from an adjoining room filled the air as the staff listened to the president's announcement on television.

That moment was truly historic for the United States and Cuba. That uplifting moment also marked the high point of the academic segment of my diplomatic career. The briefer who had stepped out to share the moment with his colleagues was one of my African American protégés, Justin Davis, the chief of the political section at what was then the U.S. Interests Section in Havana. Ten years before, I had encouraged him to pursue a career in international affairs, and now Justin not only had cleared the way for my tour group to visit the U.S. Interests Section on our eight-day visit to Cuba, he had briefed us on the significance of this historic date.

Few things in the past could match my joy in listening as Justin returned and told us U.S. ambassador Jeffrey DeLaurentis (the ambassadorial rank goes with the person even though we did not have a U.S embassy at that time), only moments before, had delivered to Cuba's deputy foreign minister the president's letter that would restore diplomatic relations and reopen permanent diplomatic missions between the United States and Cuba a few weeks from that day. Near the end of Justin's briefing, the ambassador joined us to share his enthusiasm for this long-awaited initial step toward renewed diplomatic relations after more than half a century. He spent about twelve minutes with us. We were truly honored. I thanked him for carving out a moment to meet with us on this hectic day.

At the hotel, as we had prepared for our visit to the U.S. Interests Section, we had no idea of the significance of the day ahead. Only later did we realize we could not have chosen a more poignant time in history for Justin and the ambassador to take precious time to speak to us. How well I remember having to screen the many American groups I met when they visited Senegal. I could not meet all of them, and that is why I was particularly pleased DeLaurentis made time for us.

The following day, I shared that experience in a message to a host of colleagues and to Ambassador Terence Todman's widow. The late Ambassador Todman was involved in the establishment of the U.S. Interests Section when he was assistant secretary for Latin American and Caribbean affairs at the State Department. He had been the first African American to serve as an assistant secretary. Originally from the Virgin Islands, he served as ambassador in six counties.

On July 3 I returned to Miami after an incredibly enlightening eight days in Cuba. A fascinating confluence of events had made the timing of the trip possible. On December 17, 2014, the president made his first announcement of plans to resume diplomatic relations with Cuba. He also lifted some of the restrictions for Americans traveling to Cuba. I immediately wrote an email to Justin's private email address, telling him how thrilled I was that he was working in Havana at this historic turn of events. I had seen Justin in August 2014 during the week of Ambassador Todman's memorial service at the State Department. He had just been assigned as the political counselor in Havana and was leaving in two weeks. It was his third assignment.

I first met Justin in 2004 in Washington DC, at the Stuart Educational Leadership Group's National Black Student Leadership Development Conference. The late Dr. Carroll Frances Stuart Hardy and her siblings sponsored the conference for about one thousand students of color annually until her death in 2012. Justin was then a junior at Cornell University with a host of impressive extracurricular voluntary and academic pursuits. I heard him mention that he was tutoring French-speaking Haitian students in math. I noted he was fluent in French. I suggested he consider a career in the State Department, and I told him how to apply for the Thomas R. Pickering Foreign Affairs Fellowship Program. He followed my suggestion that he attend the session I was leading on careers in foreign affairs. Justin continued to communicate with me throughout the Pickering application process, but I responded with one-line emails. I had a feeling I might be one of the panelists should he reach the interview stage, and I was right. I extended him no special preference. He stood on his own merits.

Justin now has his master's degree from Georgetown and has been a career diplomat for six years. I was moved to tears witnessing Justin's knowledge, composure, and comportment in Havana. In a very personal way, I saw my work over the past decade come full circle as Justin delivered that comprehensive briefing. I feel immensely grateful and very proud. As Justin moves forward in the Foreign Service, I am confident he will ensure our counterparts abroad have a realistic and positive view of all Americans.

By early 2015, I made the decision to go on my Cuba trip. The opportunity presented itself because I was no longer an active diplomat. All of the intricate travel details were arranged by Platinum Tours International, owned by Beverly Marshall-Luney, a former vice president of investor relations and events with the Metro Orlando Economic Development Commission. Beverly asked me to see if I could arrange a briefing at the U.S. Interests Section. Justin agreed to set it up through the cultural affairs office in the information section.

I was traveling as a private citizen on my own funds. And I was the only former diplomat among the fourteen of us. The group included some retired school principals, academic advisors, psychiatrists, a well-known artist and strong advocate for the arts, an operating-room nurse, a Department of Defense English teacher, and a medical doctor specializing in geriatrics. We teased him and said he had a laboratory right at his fingertips with our group. Our journey began on June 25 with a quite elegant Red Coach bus trip to the Crowne Plaza Miami International Hotel, where we were briefed on what to expect in Cuba. Throughout my career and even now, I seldom travel as a tourist. I often stay at the homes of Foreign Service officers. When I traveled on diplomatic business, I always had someone to meet me who knew the lay of the land. Tourists seldom gain in-depth insights into the countries they visit. At least for this trip, that would not be the case. Our tour was couched in the terms of a cultural and educational immersion. We would visit Cienfuegos, Trinidad, Santa Clara, Playa Girón, and Havana. Despite the fact that our tour was structured to present the Cuba the Castro government wanted us to see, we would also get to interact with the people of that culture in their daily lives. In those eight days, I saw more of Cuba than any active American diplomat. In the year that Justin had been stationed in Cuba, he had never seen Cienfuegos. He had never traveled beyond Havana, due to the fact that no American diplomat is allowed to leave Havana because no Cuban diplomat posted in Washington or New York is allowed to go beyond a certain distance from those two cities.

In Miami our guide, Daniel Guzman, of Puerto Rican descent, briefed us on Cuban history. Also, a Cuban American living in Miami, Annie Betancourt, a director of the League of Women Voters of Florida who served in the Florida House of Representatives from 1994 until 2002, gave us an hour-long presentation on the flight of her generation from Cuba, including the experience of her father, a university professor in Cuba before he brought his family to Florida. She is a Democrat, but she told us why so many Cubans became Republicans. She suggested that because President Jimmy Carter, a Democrat, opened the United States to Cuban immigrants, Fidel Castro decided to send the mentally ill, prostitutes, and even former prisoners to the United States. In essence, he banished the undesirables of Cuban society to the United States. The wealthy Cubans who had fled Cuba prior to this were upset with the Democrats for this opening and the majority of them decided to join the Republican Party.

After an uneventful forty-five-minute charter flight, we landed at Jaime Gonzalez International Airport at Cienfuegos, the nation's biggest seaport on the southern coast of Cuba. In a slightly air-conditioned room, we were delayed clearing customs for about an hour. That gave us our first opportunity to meet young Cuban American artists from Miami. They were going to visit their grandparents in Cuba. Thanks to their conversation with the artist in our group, we learned the cause for the hour-long delay was a breakdown in the wi-fi network. Some of us had thought it was because of the presence of the fourteen Americans arriving on our flight. I did notice that my bag had been opened, however. The TSA-approved lock was broken, but nothing was taken from my suitcase.

We stayed at the Hotel Jagua at Punta Gorda, surrounded on three sides by the Bay of Cienfuegos. All of the guests were foreign travelers. Our air-conditioned rooms were in two properties across the street from the main hotel. They appeared to be old guesthouses. The accommodations were Spartan but comfortable. The mattresses and the pillows were extremely thin, and while I don't like thick pillows, I put two of these flat pillows together in order to cushion my head a bit more.

The hotel's restaurant provided an outdoor dinner of a roasted pig. The musicians encouraged dancing. I don't eat pork, so I joined the vegetarians in our delegation, who picked at the rice, black beans, potatoes, and veggie stew and enjoyed the music and the view of the beach. We would be close to water nearly the entire trip. It's an island! And everywhere we went music was playing, absolutely beautiful music, Cuban music. Our tour included several day trips to other cities, including a bumpy three-hour coastal bus ride with a driver who knew how to navigate the roads.

This was my first trip of this kind to a communist country. In 1984 I visited Hungary, but I went as a diplomat to preview a U.S. Information Agency "blockbuster" exhibit, *Filmmaking in America*, scheduled to come to Athens, where I was then cultural attaché. While in Budapest, I had the exhibit director as my guide through the city. I was not floating around by myself as a tourist.

In Cienfuegos, with its French colonial architecture, old Detroit cars in mint condition accented the landscape. We visited a ration store where Cubans lined up for eggs, rice, beans, and other staples. Just two doors away we entered a store that sold upscale goods for those with Cuban convertible currency. Cuba has two forms of currency, the Cuban convertible peso (CUC) and the Cuban peso (CUP). The CUC is worth about one U.S. dollar, less the current exchange rate and the Cuban tax on the exchange. The CUP is worth far less. After the fall of the Soviet Union, Cuba, for a short time, used the U.S.

dollar before adopting its dual currency. Tourists might carry some Cuban pesos for very affordable street-food sales and local shops, but mostly they make payments in CUC. Cuban government wages are paid in CUP. Cubans who acquire CUC from travelers can shop in the finer stores.

I was prepared, but still somewhat annoyed, when we toured museums that depict Americans in derogatory terms. One caption under a photo described Americans as worms. The so-called Cuban Thaw has brought the reopening of embassies, but there is still a long way to go before U.S.-Cuban relations get beyond Cold War rhetoric.

On a walking tour of Cienfuegos, we stopped at the Parque Marti, the serene central park flanked by the provincial government buildings, the Palacio del Ayuntamiento and the Arco de Triunfo. We ventured to Teatro Tomas Terry, a theater with a façade of gold-leafed mosaics, Carrera marble, and hand-carved Cuban hardwoods. We window shopped along El Bulevar and enjoyed an orchestra performance. One day we lunched at Casa Enrique, a private guesthouse where the owners told us stories of their private enterprises. For dinner we dined at another private business, an open-air Havana restaurant where the specialty is slow-roasted chicken.

Our tour, however, presented us with contrasts. One morning we were given the Cuban perspective of the Bay of Pigs invasion as told at a museum at Playa Girón, a beach village on Cuba's southern coast that was one of the two landing spots where CIA-trained Cuban exiles launched their failed effort to overthrow Fidel Castro in April 1961. The village is in the province of Matanzas, "slaughter" in Spanish. The Museo Girón is near the invaders' last stand. The botched invasion was planned by the CIA and endorsed by outgoing president Dwight D. Eisenhower. President John Kennedy gave his approval, but he balked at using U.S. forces. The failed invasion was a fiasco and pushed Castro into seeking trade, military, and political ties with the Soviet Union.

At the museum, the Cuban government takes great pride in showing photographs of the captured invaders and displaying captured weapons and equipment. The museum's theme cannot be missed: the "imperial" government of the United States had been taught a lesson. The museum shows a short film of the "first defeat of U.S. imperialism in the Americas." Granted, many of the ugly comments are deserved, but as an American, I found it disturbing.

Upon my return from Cuba, I found hope that at least some of that tension is easing. In August 2015 John Kerry became the first sitting secretary of state to visit Cuba since those troubled times. (He was actually the first since 1945.) On August 14, the day after Fidel Castro's eighty-ninth birthday, Kerry participated in raising the American flag at the embassy. He had been a seventeen year old when he watched on a black-and-white television set as President John Kennedy, alerting the nation that the Soviets were shipping nuclear warheads to Cuba, spoke of Cuba as an "imprisoned island." The year was 1962, a year after the Bay of Pigs fiasco had led to the Kennedy administration's ban on all imports of Cuban products in an attempt to isolate the communist nation only miles off the southern tip of Florida.

The Cuban Missile Crisis was, perhaps, the height of the Cold War. At midday on January 4, 1961, three U.S. Marines lowered the American flag at the embassy. Those same Marines, James Tracy, Francis East, and Larry Morris, were back in Havana on August 14, 2015, to hand Old Glory to three young Marines who would raise the flag once again. With the reopening of the embassy in Cuba, the United States now has diplomatic relations with 195 countries. That Kerry delivered a portion of his speech in Spanish reinforces my mantra about the importance of speaking another language. Later that day, Kerry strolled the streets of Havana, greeted the enthusiastic crowds, and also viewed the vintage American cars lining streets bordered by sixteenth- and seventeenth-century colonial architecture.

On our tour, we saw communities built for the rich and famous that no longer house the rich and famous. Communities of the poor are in great disarray, but government buildings remain in mint condition. I found that very interesting. Mausoleo Che Guevara in Santa Clara is in pristine condition. At the government ministry of this and ministry of that, there's no mildew, no deterioration, everything looks like the buildings in Washington DC. (And I am mindful that blight and poverty are not unique to Cuba. The greatest U.S. cities have their own pockets of economic decay.)

One morning trip took us to botanical gardens founded by Harvard professors and an American sugarcane planter for research on sugarcane, before we toured a sugarcane factory and estate. The afternoon took us to the Trinidad neighborhood, with its winding cobblestone streets and pastel-hued houses, another UNESCO World Heritage Site. Mixed with Cuba's best-preserved colonial beauty were rationing stores for staples, another example of the complex reality of today's Cuba. Cubans living with food rationing walk by fine restaurants catering to tourists.

Hospitals and medical schools appeared to be run down from the outside. I realized, however, that the façades of the buildings did not indicate the quality of the instruction going on inside. The latest gadgetry is often not necessary to treat people for an illness. The Cubans seem to have positive doctor-patient relationships, which indicates their approach is effective. Cuban doctors are reputed to be among the best in the world. Recently, Cuban doctors helped stem the Ebola crisis in West Africa.

A former boss who also has taken a restricted tour of Cuba's museums, artists' galleries, and dance studios found them all interesting, but he doubts he saw much of how life is in Cuba. "To get to the last three feet to talk to an everyday Cuban is a challenge," said Michael Eisenstadt, who offered sobering reflections on his trip to Cuba. He was director of the European Area of the former U. S. Information Agency. I reported to him when I was the desk officer for Greece, Turkey, and Cyprus in the late 1980s. Eisenstadt spent the majority of his career in Iron Curtain countries. "Cuban communism has brought free education and the literacy rate is high," he noted. "Medical care is free, but it is basic medical care, concentrating on preventive medicine. The Cuban government claims there is no crime." Yet he observed first-floor metal grates on most houses and other buildings. Theft from government institutions that he observed in other communist countries is endemic in Cuba. The government takes 90 percent of farm crops. Fruit and vegetable markets are expensive. Most of the famed old cars are taxis used for tourists.

"Since the average salary in Cuba is thirty nonconvertible pesos, giving the hotel doorman a tip of two or three convertible pesos is giving him two or three months' salary," Eisenstadt pointed out. "Politically, everyone is afraid to speak freely. Several people we spoke with said things that ended with a plea not to tell anyone what was said," he said, adding, "Every street in every town has a political committee that monitors what goes on with all the neighbors."

Justin Davis, whose embassy responsibilities include investigating human rights violations, is well aware of the Cuban government's efforts to thwart exposure of human rights abuses. Eisenstadt notes that only the tourist hotels have the London feed of CNN and other non-Cuban channels. Foreign newspapers and magazines are absent, except for the ones left behind by tourists. Internet access is limited and expensive. But Eisenstadt did find Cuba's landscape and coast beautiful.

One of my travel companions, Percy Luney, vice president for education and workforce development at Space Florida in Orlando, came home with sympathy for the Cuban people and even its government. He rejects the notion that Americans' attitude toward Cuba comes down to a choice of either opening up Cuba to an American economic onslaught or continuing to view all things Cuban as evil and bad. "I found plenty of opportunities to interact with regular Cubans on our trip and, for the most part, they seemed better off than most other citizens in third world democracies that I have visited in Africa," he stated.

Luney added, "The Cuban government's blight and the conditions faced by its people are directly related to the U.S. foreign policy and the embargo." The United States, he notes, supported Batista and his Mafia cronies in the pre-Castro era. The Cuban situation is much more complex than simple black-and-white approaches to problem solving.

The future of Cuba is far more positive than I had thought. I experienced many positive things in Cuban culture and Cuban society.

With the opening of the embassy, I anticipate significant cultural exchanges, even while Raul Castro is still in power. People-to-people exchanges are nothing new. Eisenhower, the president who closed the embassy, also is the president who instituted America's cultural outreach to the world.

Yet even with the reopening of the embassy and the anticipated lifting of the U.S. embargo, I do not believe that the current government will allow Starbucks, KFC, and McDonald's to proliferate on the streets of major cities. And I think that it will take some time for American businesses to invest in Cuba. Only time will tell if investors will have fewer restraints than in the past. Jay Leno and others who collect vintage cars might figure out a way to get some of the refurbished vehicles to the United States as antiques.

The older generation of the rebellion might still support the Castro regime, but the younger generation is very pro-American. One young man told us he was thrilled we were there. I think he was speaking from his heart. He was thirtyish, a senior violinist with a group of modern chamber musicians. Confirming forty-plus years of what I've been doing, he told us he believes in cultural exchanges through music and the arts. That is what we used to do behind the Iron Curtain, why we had exhibits, why we were involved in cultural exchange when we could not otherwise communicate because of political differences. He was giving the same type of speech I used to give as cultural attaché in the posts I had early on in my life. I could not have felt more vindicated. This young artist exemplified our belief that arts and culture continue to have value. No matter how strong our political differences, there are few people not moved by the sound of an aria or a chorus in a song or a beautiful piece of art. Almost our entire group was moved to tears when this artist played "Shenandoah" for us.

In Cuba I found instances of openness I did not expect, even with some of the older generation. They had lived through half a century of Cold War estrangement. At a senior center, we met Cubans who would have been in their twenties and thirties when Castro came to power. The hosts carried themselves with dignity, grace, and elegance. The ladies reminded me of my mother's friends. Their white hair was perfectly coiffed. They wore attractively tailored, light-colored cotton blouses with traditional peasant-like skirts, and they all had their fans. The men were well attired in the traditional Cuban shirts and short-brimmed straw hats. They ranged in age from seventy-three to eighty-nine. The lovely ladies explained that when they were young and constantly surrounded by chaperones they used the fans to communicate with men they wanted to date, or not date. They introduced us to their classical dance, which they created so they would no longer have to do classic European waltzes that the colonialists had taught them. Their version of the waltz is a little slower, using, of course, Cuban music. It is called *danzón*. It is absolutely beautiful to watch. I also learned that the cha-cha originated in Cuba, and, of course, I learned we did not do it right.

On July 1 we arrived at the U.S. Interests Section about thirty minutes before our scheduled 9:00 a.m. briefing to give us time to go through three levels of security. As security collected our passports, purses, and cameras, I was reminded of my days in Istanbul when the Marine guards confiscated film from two lovely old ladies in tennis shoes who were taking pictures within the embassy.

After clearing security, we sat in the lobby. I recall a feeling of sadness as I looked around the stark surroundings. Every other embassy where I worked was decorated with colorful photos of joint projects between America and the host country. In this lobby there were only a few faded photos of landscapes and the traditional pictures of the secretary of state and the president. There was a small display of agricultural projects that might have been done in Cuba with USAID money decades ago. As I took in the scene of just how removed that lobby was from Cuban life, others in my group noticed a gray-haired man in a suit flanked by security guards passing through the lobby. It was the ambassador, leaving with the president's letter to deliver to the Cuban Foreign Ministry. Ambassador DeLaurentis had been in Cuba when the United States returned young Elián González to his father. He had been in Cuba during the Mariel boatlift. What better person for the White House to send as its chief of mission as relations warmed? At that time, however, we had no idea that a threshold moment in history had arrived.

A short time later, we were seated in the briefing room. It looked about as inviting as a hospital. Again, our briefing rooms in other countries absolutely glitter with images of American involvement in that country. But we could not do that in Cuba. Julio Llopiz, a Foreign Service national, gave us a wonderful briefing on what had happened during our days out of the loop, and then Justin started his briefing. He began, "I'd like to tell you about this lady. I met her at a conference many years ago. When she heard me speaking French, she told me I should consider a career in the State Department. I took her advice and applied for a Pickering scholarship . . . and I walk into the room for my final interview with three ambassadors and she's one of the panelists. . . . I would not be here if not for her."

My career highlights include awards from the Greek government and the former Turkish prime minister Suleyman Demirel and the Director General's Cup, one of the most prestigious honors for former Foreign Service officers. Yet nothing was as satisfying and gratifying as that day. I have taught a number of young women and men at UCF. As I mentioned earlier, several have gained internships in Washington or abroad. Others have received critical language scholarships and Pickering and Rangel Fellowships. Others have attended the London School of Economics, the University of Kent, and Marburg University in Germany. A few have taught English in China, Korea, or Japan or continued their language study in these countries. I am very proud of them, but I saw my life's work come full circle that morning.

Justin Davis briefs the ambassador on political issues every morning. He is also the human rights officer. And this young man talks about how his life is not what it might have been if we had never met. Justin let me know that the next generation is not lost. These young men and women have a genuine commitment to diplomacy. They understand that commitment requires sensitivity to other cultures and the patience not to look for instant gratification. My time was well spent. That moment allowed me to experience that I have lived a life of authenticity.

Index

Italicized figure numbers refer to illustrations following page 74.

HLET = Harriet Lee Elam-Thomas.

Related ADST-DACOR Book Series Titles

Fifty Years of U.S. Africa Policy: Reflections of Assistant Secretaries for African Affairs and U.S. Embassy Officials
Claudia E. Anyaso, Ed.

Mossy Memoir of a Rolling Stone
Thompson Buchanan

Intervening in Africa: Superpower Peacemaking in a Troubled Continent
Herman J. Cohen

The Mind of the African Strongman: Conversations with Dictators, Statesmen, and Father Figures
Herman J. Cohen

Inventing Public Diplomacy: The Story of the United States Information Agency
Wilson Dizard Sr.

Ambassador to a Small World: Letters from Chad
Christopher Goldthwait

Behind Embassy Walls: The Life and Times of an American Diplomat
Brandon Grove

Paying Calls in Shangri-La: Scenes from a Woman's Life in American Diplomacy
Judith M. Heimann

High-Value Target: Countering al Qaeda in Yemen
Edmund J. Hull

American Ambassadors: The Past, Present, and Future of America's Diplomats
Dennis C. Jett

The Architecture of Diplomacy: Building America's Embassies
Jane C. Loeffler

Witness to a Changing World
David D. Newsom

Memoirs of a Foreign Service Arabist
Richard B. Parker

Practicing Public Diplomacy: A Cold War Odyssey
Yale Richmond

The Craft of Political Analysis for Diplomats
Raymond F. Smith

In Those Days: A Diplomat Remembers
James W. Spain

A Long Way from Runnemede: One Woman's Foreign Service Journey
Theresa Tull

Abroad for Her Country: Tales of a Pioneer Woman Ambassador in the U.S. Foreign Service
Jean Wilkowski

Peregrina: Unexpected Adventures of an American Consul
Ginny Carson Young

For a complete list of series titles, visit adst.org/publications.